The Official Ninja Foodi 2-in-1 Flip Toaster Cookbook for Beginners

Fast, Simple, and Tasty Recipes for the Ninja Foodi 2-in-1 Flip Toaster, featuring Toast, Pizza Bagel, Thick-cut Bread, Chicken Nuggets, Sandwich, Defrost, Bake, Broil, and Reheat!

Denevieve Ishcroft

© **Copyright 2023 Denevieve Ishcroft - All Rights Reserved.**

It is in no way legal to reproduce, duplicate, or transmit any part of this document by either electronic means or in printed format. Recording of this publication is strictly prohibited, and any storage of this material is not allowed unless with written permission from the publisher. All rights reserved.

The information provided herein is stated to be truthful and consistent, in that any liability, regarding inattention or otherwise, by any usage or abuse of any policies, processes, or directions contained within is the solitary and complete responsibility of the recipient reader. Under no circumstances will any legal liability or blame be held against the publisher for any reparation, damages, or monetary loss due to the information herein, either directly or indirectly.

Respective authors own all copyrights not held by the publisher.

Legal Notice:

This book is copyright protected. This is only for personal use. You cannot amend, distribute, sell, use, quote or paraphrase any part of the content within this book without the consent of the author or copyright owner. Legal action will be pursued if this is breached.

Disclaimer Notice:

Please note the information contained within this document is for educational and entertainment purposes only. Every attempt has been made to provide accurate, up-to-date, reliable, and complete information. No warranties of any kind are expressed or implied. Readers acknowledge that the author is not engaging in the rendering of legal, financial, medical or professional advice.

By reading this document, the reader agrees that under no circumstances are we responsible for any losses, direct or indirect, which are incurred as a result of the use of information contained within this document, including, but not limited to, errors, omissions, or inaccuracies.

Table of Contents

Introduction ·· 5

Chapter 1: Breakfast and Brunch ················· 21

Chapter 2: Chicken and Poultry ·················· 32

Chapter 3: Beef, Pork and Lamb·················· 42

Chapter 4: Fish and Seafood ······················· 54

Chapter 5: Vegetables and Vegetarian Mains · 65

Chapter 6: Appetizers and Snacks··············· 80

Chapter 7: Desserts and Baked Goods ·········· 94

Appendix recipe Index ······························· 109

INTRODUCTION

Understanding of Your Ninja Foodi 2-In-1 Flip Toaster

The Ninja Foodi Flip Toaster is a revolutionary kitchen appliance that combines the functionality of a toaster and a compact toaster oven in one convenient and space-saving design. Let's delve deeper into its features, capabilities, and how it enhances your cooking experience.

Design and Build:

The Ninja Foodi Flip Toaster boasts a compact and sleek design, making it an ideal addition to any kitchen with limited counter space. The 2-in-1 flip functionality is a standout feature, allowing users to seamlessly switch between toaster and oven modes. The flip mechanism is intuitive, providing a hassle-free transition, making it a versatile and efficient appliance.

Versatile Cooking Functions:

This appliance is not limited to traditional toasting; it offers a wide array of cooking functions. In toaster mode, users can enjoy the convenience of Toast, Bagel, and Defrost functions, ensuring perfectly toasted bread and bagels every time. The 7 shade settings provide customization, allowing you to achieve your desired level of toasting.

When flipped down to unlock oven mode, the Ninja Foodi Flip Toaster transforms into a capable baking and broiling appliance. The Bake function is perfect for baking cookies, muffins, or small casseroles. The Broil function allows for quick and efficient cooking of meats and vegetables, giving a crispy finish. Reheat function ensures leftovers taste as good as fresh.

Rapid Oven Technology:

One of the standout features of the Ninja Foodi Flip Toaster is its Rapid Oven Technology. With the ability to reach up to 400°F of heat and no preheating required, it cooks up to 35% faster than a full-size electric oven. This not only saves time but also contributes to energy efficiency, making it an eco-friendly choice for those conscious of their environmental impact.

Easy Cleaning:

The inclusion of a crumb tray in both toaster and oven modes is a thoughtful design element. This feature ensures that any crumbs generated during toasting or cooking are collected, making cleaning a breeze. The removable crumb tray can be easily emptied and washed, maintaining hygiene and preventing any buildup that may affect the appliance's performance over time.

Perfect Toast:

The Ninja Foodi Flip Toaster takes pride in delivering more even toasting compared to traditional toasters. The front-to-back evenness ensures that every slice of bread or bagel is toasted uniformly, enhancing the overall taste and texture of your breakfast or snack.

Wider Slot for Artisan Breads:

The appliance's 70% wider slot, compared to traditional toasters, is a game-changer. It accommodates long artisan breads and bakery-style bagels with ease, catering to diverse preferences. The ability to customize the Toast and Bagel functions with 7 shade settings further allows users to achieve the perfect level of doneness, whether they prefer a lightly toasted or a more golden-brown finish.

In summary, the Ninja Foodi Flip Toaster is a versatile and efficient kitchen appliance that combines the convenience of a toaster and the functionality of a compact toaster oven. With its innovative flip functionality, rapid oven technology, and easy-to-clean design, it caters to the needs of busy individuals and families who seek a reliable and space-saving solution for their cooking requirements.

2-In-1 Flip Functionality

The Ninja Foodi Flip Toaster introduces a revolutionary 2-in-1 flip functionality, seamlessly combining the convenience of a toaster and the versatility of a compact toaster oven within one small footprint. This innovative design not only saves counter space but also opens up a world of cooking possibilities for users seeking efficiency and variety in their kitchen appliances.

Versatility Redefined:

The key feature of the 2-in-1 flip functionality lies in its ability to effortlessly transition between toaster and oven modes. When flipped up, the appliance operates as a traditional toaster, offering functions such as Toast, Bagel, and

Defrost. This mode caters to those who enjoy their morning toast or crave the crispy exterior of a perfectly toasted bagel.

Upon flipping down, the appliance transforms into a compact toaster oven, unlocking a range of cooking methods including Bake, Broil, and Reheat. This transition is smooth and quick, allowing users to seamlessly switch between toasting and baking without the need for multiple appliances. The versatility of this flip functionality expands the range of culinary creations users can explore, making it a go-to solution for various meals and snacks.

Space-Efficient Design:

The compact footprint of the Ninja Foodi Flip Toaster is a game-changer for kitchens with limited space. The 2-in-1 flip functionality eliminates the need for separate toaster and toaster oven units, providing a space-saving solution without compromising on capabilities. The vertical flip design not only saves counter space but also adds a modern and sleek aesthetic to the kitchen.

Users can enjoy the benefits of a toaster and a toaster oven without cluttering their countertops. The flip mechanism is designed for ease of use, ensuring a hassle-free transition between modes. The thoughtful engineering of the flip functionality aligns with the contemporary kitchen's demand for multi-functional, space-saving appliances.

Enhanced Toasting Experience:

In toaster mode, the Ninja Foodi Flip Toaster brings an advanced toasting experience to the table. The appliance boasts a 70% wider slot compared to traditional slot toasters, accommodating long artisan breads and bakery-style bagels with ease. This wider slot ensures even toasting, addressing the common issue of uneven browning in traditional toasters.

Furthermore, the customizable Toast and Bagel functions come with 7 shade settings, allowing users to achieve their preferred level of doneness. Whether it's a lightly toasted slice or a perfectly crispy bagel, the Ninja Foodi Flip Toaster caters to individual preferences, elevating the toasting experience.

Efficient Baking and Broiling:

The flip-down toaster oven mode introduces a new dimension to cooking with Bake and Broil functions. The compact oven, powered by 1500 watts, utilizes rapid oven technology that reaches temperatures up to 400°F without the need for preheating. This feature is a game-changer for those seeking quick and efficient cooking, enabling up to 35% faster cooking times compared to a full-size electric oven.

The compact oven capacity is designed to accommodate various dishes, from 2 slices of thick-cut bread to 16 chicken nuggets, an 8" open-face sandwich, or 2 full-size pizza bagels. This flexibility in capacity ensures that users can prepare a wide range of meals, from snacks to individual portions, making the Ninja Foodi Flip Toaster a versatile and indispensable kitchen companion.

In conclusion, the 2-in-1 flip functionality of the Ninja Foodi Flip Toaster redefines kitchen efficiency and versatility. By seamlessly integrating toaster and toaster oven capabilities into a single, compact appliance, it addresses the modern kitchen's need for space-saving solutions without compromising on performance. The enhanced toasting experience, efficient baking and broiling, and easy cleaning make this appliance a standout choice for users seeking a versatile and convenient kitchen companion.

What To Cook in The Ninja Foodi Flip Toaster

The Ninja Foodi Flip Toaster is a versatile kitchen appliance that combines the functions of a toaster and a compact toaster oven. Its 2-in-1 flip functionality allows you to toast bread and bagels or switch to oven mode for baking, broiling, and reheating. Here are some exciting recipes and ideas to make the most out of your Ninja Foodi Flip Toaster:

- Artisan Toasts and Bagels:
  Take advantage of the toaster mode by creating delicious artisan toasts or

perfectly toasted bagels. The 70% wider slot accommodates longer bread slices and bakery-style bagels. Customize the toasting level with the 7 shade settings for your preferred crispiness.

- Mini Pizzas:

  In oven mode, you can quickly prepare mini pizzas for a snack or light meal. Use pre-made pizza crusts or English muffins as the base, add your favorite toppings, and let the Ninja Foodi Flip Toaster bake them to perfection.

- Open-Face Sandwiches:

  Utilize the compact oven capacity to make open-face sandwiches. Toast the bread in toaster mode, then switch to oven mode to melt cheese and warm up toppings, creating a delightful and customizable open-face sandwich.

- Chicken Nuggets or Wings:

  The toaster oven is perfect for quickly cooking small portions of frozen or fresh chicken nuggets or wings. Achieve a crispy texture without the need for preheating, thanks to the rapid oven technology.

- Quick Baked Desserts:

  Experiment with easy-to-make desserts in the toaster oven. Try baking individual portions of cookies, brownies, or even small cakes. The rapid oven technology ensures swift and even cooking for your sweet treats.

- Reheating Leftovers:

  Use the reheating function to revive leftovers without sacrificing their texture. Whether it's pizza, pasta, or casseroles, the toaster oven can efficiently reheat your meals with minimal effort.

- Garlic Bread or Toasted Sandwiches:

    Make flavorful garlic bread by toasting the slices in toaster mode, then switch to oven mode to melt butter and garlic on top. You can also assemble and toast delicious toasted sandwiches with melted cheese and your favorite fillings.

- Mini Frittatas or Quiches:

    Explore the baking capabilities of the Ninja Foodi Flip Toaster by whipping up mini frittatas or quiches. Beat eggs, add your preferred veggies, cheese, or meats, and let the toaster oven cook these individual-sized delights.

- Toaster Strudels or Pastries:

    Enjoy flaky and golden toaster pastries or strudels in toaster mode. The even toasting ensures a delightful crunch, and the wider slot accommodates a variety of pastry sizes.

- Quick Roasted Vegetables:

    Harness the oven mode for quick-roasting vegetables. Toss your favorite veggies in olive oil and seasonings, then roast until tender and caramelized, offering a healthy and flavorful side dish.

In summary, the Ninja Foodi Flip Toaster offers a wide range of cooking possibilities, from traditional toasting to baking, broiling, and reheating. Get creative in the kitchen and explore the various functions to discover new and exciting recipes tailored to your preferences.

Tips and Tricks for Making the Most of Your Toaster

The Ninja Foodi Flip Toaster is a kitchen powerhouse, and with a few tips and tricks, you can maximize its potential and efficiency. Here's a guide to help you make the most out of your versatile appliance:

- Preheat Strategically:

    While the toaster oven boasts rapid oven technology, preheating can enhance certain recipes. For baked goods like cookies and cakes, a short preheat can ensure even cooking. However, for quick snacks like toast or reheating leftovers, you can skip the preheating process.

- Utilize Multi-Functionality:

    Experiment with the toaster's various functions. Switch between toaster and oven mode based on your cooking needs. From toasting and baking to broiling and reheating, the Ninja Foodi Flip Toaster is designed to handle it all.

- Customize Toasting Levels:

  Take advantage of the seven shade settings to customize your toasting preferences. Whether you prefer a light golden brown or a deep, crispy toast, the Ninja Foodi Flip Toaster allows you to achieve the perfect level of doneness.

- Optimize Oven Mode for Efficiency:

  When using the toaster oven for baking or roasting, maximize efficiency by placing items close to the heating element. This ensures that your food cooks evenly and takes full advantage of the rapid oven technology.

- Rotate and Monitor:

  For recipes that require even cooking, like cookies or mini pizzas, rotate the baking tray halfway through the cooking time. Additionally, keep an eye on your food, especially during the first few uses, to familiarize yourself with the appliance's cooking dynamics.

- Use Parchment Paper or Foil:

  Line the toaster oven tray with parchment paper or aluminum foil for easy cleanup and to prevent sticking. This is particularly helpful when baking cookies, roasting vegetables, or reheating messy foods.

- Size Matters:

  Be mindful of the compact oven capacity. While it accommodates a variety of foods, avoid overloading the toaster oven to ensure proper air circulation and even cooking. For larger batches, consider using a conventional oven.

- Experiment with Temperature and Time:

  Get to know your toaster oven's temperature settings and cooking times. Since it cooks faster than a full-size oven, you may need to adjust temperatures or reduce cooking times for certain recipes.

- Clean Regularly:

  To maintain optimal performance, clean the crumb tray regularly. This simple step ensures that the toaster and oven modes function efficiently and prevents any unwanted odors or smoke during cooking.

- Explore Accessories:

  Some toaster ovens come with additional accessories like baking pans or air fryer baskets. Check if your Ninja Foodi Flip Toaster has compatible accessories to expand its capabilities, allowing you to air fry, dehydrate, or roast with ease.

In conclusion, the Ninja Foodi Flip Toaster is a versatile appliance that can streamline your cooking process. By understanding its functions, experimenting with recipes, and incorporating these tips and tricks, you'll be able to make the most out of this 2-in-1 toaster and oven, creating a wide array of delicious meals and snacks with ease.

Flip Toaster Troubleshooting

The Ninja Foodi Flip Toaster is a versatile appliance designed to make your toasting and baking experience seamless. However, like any electronic device, it may encounter issues from time to time. Here's a comprehensive guide to troubleshooting common problems with the Flip Toaster:

Power Issues:

- Symptom: The toaster is not turning on.
- Solution: Ensure that the toaster is plugged into a working power outlet. Check the power cord for any visible damage. If the issue persists, try plugging the toaster into a different outlet. If the problem continues, there might be an internal electrical issue, and you should contact Ninja customer support.

Uneven Toasting:

- Symptom: The toaster is not toasting bread evenly.
- Solution: Make sure that you are using bread slices of similar thickness. Adjust the browning control to a higher setting for a darker toast or a lower setting for a lighter one. If the uneven toasting persists, it could be due to a malfunction in the heating elements. Cleaning the toaster thoroughly, especially removing any accumulated crumbs, might improve performance. If the issue persists, contact Ninja customer support for further assistance.

Functionality Issues:

- Symptom: The toaster is not switching between modes or functions.
- Solution: Check if the flip mechanism is working correctly. Ensure that the toaster is securely locked in either toaster or oven mode. If the problem persists, there might be an issue with the internal mechanism or sensor. Avoid forcing the toaster into a mode; instead, contact Ninja customer support for guidance.

Overheating:

- Symptom: The toaster becomes excessively hot during use.
- Solution: Check for any obstruction around the toaster that could be blocking ventilation. Ensure that the toaster is placed on a flat, heat-resistant surface. If the toaster continues to overheat, it might be due to a malfunction in the thermostat or other internal components. Stop using the appliance immediately and contact Ninja customer support for assistance.

Inconsistent Cooking in Oven Mode:

- Symptom: Food is not cooking evenly in oven mode.
- Solution: Ensure that you are following the recommended cooking times and temperatures for the specific food you are preparing. If the issue persists, it could be related to a problem with the oven's heating elements or thermostat. Try cleaning the oven interior and checking for any signs of damage. If the problem continues, contact Ninja customer support.

Error Codes:

- Symptom: The toaster displays error codes.
- Solution: Refer to the user manual for a list of error codes and their meanings. If you encounter an error code, follow the recommended steps in the manual to troubleshoot the specific issue. If the problem persists or if you cannot find a solution in the manual, contact Ninja customer support.

Crumb Tray Issues:

- Symptom: The crumb tray is difficult to remove or reinsert.
- Solution: Ensure that the toaster is cool before attempting to remove or reinsert the crumb tray. If the tray is still difficult to manage, check for any crumbs or debris that might be obstructing its movement. Clean the crumb tray and its surrounding area thoroughly. If the issue persists, contact Ninja customer support for assistance.

In conclusion, troubleshooting the Ninja Foodi Flip Toaster involves a systematic approach to identify and address specific issues. Always refer to the user manual for guidance and, if necessary, seek assistance from Ninja customer support to ensure the longevity and optimal performance of your appliance.

Chapter 1: Breakfast and Brunch

Avocado Toast with Poached Eggs

Prep Time: 10 Minutes Cook Time: 15 Minutes Serves: 2-4

Ingredients:

- 4 slices whole-grain bread
- 2 ripe avocados
- 4 large eggs
- Salt and pepper to taste
- Optional toppings: cherry tomatoes, red pepper flakes, or feta cheese

Directions:

1. Flip up for toaster mode and heat to 400°F.
2. Place two bread slices on the toaster rack and toast until golden brown, about 4 minutes.
3. While the bread is toasting, mash the avocados in a bowl and season with salt and pepper.
4. Flip down for oven mode. Fill a shallow oven-safe dish with water. Crack each egg into the dish, leaving space between them. Bake until the egg whites are set but the yolks are still runny, about 8-10 minutes.
5. Spread the mashed avocado on the toasted bread slices. Carefully place a poached egg on each slice. Add optional toppings if desired.
6. Arrange the avocado toast on a platter and serve immediately.

Nutritional Value (Amount per Serving):

Calories: 439; Fat: 28.01; Carb: 37.58; Protein: 13.93

Berry-Stuffed French Toast

Prep Time: 15 Minutes Cook Time: 20 Minutes Serves: 4

Ingredients:

- 8 slices of thick-cut bread
- 1 cup mixed berries (strawberries, blueberries, raspberries)
- 4 large eggs
- 1 cup milk
- 1 teaspoon vanilla extract
- Maple syrup for serving

Directions:

1. Flip up for toaster mode and heat to 400°F.
2. Cut a slit in each slice of bread to create a pocket. Stuff each pocket with a handful of mixed berries.
3. In a bowl, whisk together eggs, milk, and vanilla extract.

4. Dip each stuffed bread slice into the egg mixture, coating both sides. Place on the toaster rack and toast until golden brown, about 8-10 minutes.
5. Drizzle with maple syrup and serve warm.

Nutritional Value (Amount per Serving):

Calories: 378; Fat: 13.71; Carb: 54.23; Protein: 9.26

Spinach and Feta Breakfast Wrap

Prep Time: 10 Minutes   Cook Time: 15 Minutes   Serves: 2

Ingredients:

- 4 large eggs, beaten
- 1 cup fresh spinach, chopped
- 1/2 cup crumbled feta cheese
- 2 whole wheat tortillas
- Salt and pepper to taste

Directions:

1. Flip up for toaster mode and heat to 400°F.
2. In a skillet over medium heat, scramble the beaten eggs. Add chopped spinach and cook until wilted. Season with salt and pepper.
3. Lay out the tortillas and divide the scrambled eggs and spinach between them. Sprinkle crumbled feta cheese on top.
4. Roll up the tortillas, folding in the sides, and place them on the toaster rack. Toast for about 5 minutes or until the wraps are heated through and slightly crispy.

Nutritional Value (Amount per Serving):

Calories: 348; Fat: 21.11; Carb: 24.24; Protein: 15.6

Blueberry Almond Breakfast Bread

Prep Time: 15 Minutes   Cook Time: 20 Minutes   Serves: 4-6

Ingredients:

- 1 cup fresh or frozen blueberries
- 1 cup almond flour
- 1 cup all-purpose flour
- 1/2 cup sugar
- 1 teaspoon baking powder
- 1/2 teaspoon salt
- 2 large eggs
- 1/2 cup milk
- 1/4 cup melted butter
- 1 teaspoon almond extract

Directions:

1. Flip down for oven mode, choose the Bake function and heat to 375°F.
2. In one bowl, whisk together almond flour, all-purpose flour, sugar, baking powder, and salt. In another bowl, beat the eggs, then add milk, melted

butter, and almond extract.
3. Add the wet ingredients to the dry ingredients, stirring until just combined. Gently fold in the blueberries.
4. Pour the batter into a greased loaf pan and bake for 18-20 minutes or until a toothpick inserted comes out clean.

Nutritional Value (Amount per Serving):

Calories: 268; Fat: 12.5; Carb: 34.82; Protein: 4.76

Apple Walnut Breakfast Bread

Prep Time: 15 Minutes   Cook Time: 25 Minutes   Serves: 4-6

Ingredients:

- 2 cups peeled and diced apples
- 2 cups all-purpose flour
- 1 teaspoon baking soda
- 1/2 teaspoon baking powder
- 1/2 teaspoon cinnamon
- 1/4 teaspoon salt
- 2 large eggs
- 1/2 cup vegetable oil
- 1 cup sugar
- 1 teaspoon vanilla extract
- 1/2 cup chopped walnuts

Directions:

1. Flip down for oven mode, choose the Bake function and heat to 350°F.
2. In one bowl, whisk together flour, baking soda, baking powder, cinnamon, and salt. In another bowl, beat the eggs, then add oil, sugar, and vanilla extract.
3. Add the wet ingredients to the dry ingredients, stirring until just combined. Fold in the diced apples and chopped walnuts.
4. Pour the batter into a greased loaf pan and bake for 22-25 minutes or until a toothpick inserted comes out clean.

Nutritional Value (Amount per Serving):

Calories: 548; Fat: 29.39; Carb: 66.02; Protein: 7.59

Veggie Breakfast Burritos

Prep Time: 20 Minutes   Cook Time: 15 Minutes   Serves: 4

Ingredients:

- 4 large tortillas
- 6 large eggs, scrambled
- 1 cup black beans, drained and rinsed
- 1 cup diced bell peppers (assorted colors)

- 1 cup diced tomatoes
- 1 cup shredded cheddar cheese
- Salsa and guacamole for serving

Directions:

1. Flip up your Toaster Oven to Toast mode and set the temperature to 400°F.
2. Place tortillas on the toaster rack and toast until they are warm and slightly crispy.
3. In a pan, scramble the eggs until just set.
4. In a bowl, mix together black beans, diced bell peppers, diced tomatoes, and shredded cheddar cheese.
5. Divide the scrambled eggs among the warm tortillas, top with the veggie and cheese mixture.
6. Fold in the sides of each tortilla and then roll up tightly to form a burrito.
7. Flip down your toaster oven to Oven mode. Place the burritos on the rack and bake for 5-7 minutes or until the cheese is melted.
8. Serve with salsa and guacamole on the side.

Nutritional Value (Amount per Serving):

Calories: 382; Fat: 11.01; Carb: 47.42; Protein: 24.09

Veggie Omelette Muffins

Prep Time: 10 Minutes   Cook Time: 15 Minutes   Serves: 4

Ingredients:

- 6 large eggs
- 1/4 cup milk
- Salt and pepper, to taste
- 1/2 cup diced bell peppers
- 1/2 cup diced tomatoes
- 1/4 cup diced onions
- 1/2 cup shredded cheese (cheddar or your choice)
- Cooking spray

Directions:

1. Ensure the Flip Toaster Oven is in oven mode (flipped down) and heat to 375°F.
2. In a bowl, whisk together eggs, milk, salt, and pepper until well combined.
3. Add diced bell peppers, tomatoes, onions, and shredded cheese to the egg mixture. Mix well.
4. Lightly spray the muffin cups with cooking spray.
5. Pour the egg and vegetable mixture evenly into muffin cups.
6. Bake for 12-15 minutes or until the muffins are set and lightly golden.

7. Remove the Veggie Omelette Muffins from the Flip Toaster Oven and let them cool for a few minutes before serving.

Nutritional Value (Amount per Serving):

Calories: 170; Fat: 12.38; Carb: 5.59; Protein: 9.24

Baked Banana Nut Oatmeal

Prep Time: 10 Minutes   Cook Time: 25 Minutes   Serves: 4

Ingredients:

- 2 cups old-fashioned oats
- 1/2 cup chopped nuts (walnuts or pecans)
- 2 ripe bananas, mashed
- 2 cups milk
- 1/4 cup maple syrup
- 1 teaspoon vanilla extract
- 1/2 teaspoon cinnamon
- Pinch of salt

Directions:

1. Ensure the Flip Toaster Oven is in oven mode (flipped down) and heat to 375°F.
2. In a large bowl, combine oats, chopped nuts, mashed bananas, milk, maple syrup, vanilla extract, cinnamon, and a pinch of salt.
3. Pour the oatmeal mixture into a greased baking dish.
4. Bake for 20-25 minutes or until the edges are golden brown and the center is set.
5. Allow the baked banana nut oatmeal to cool for a few minutes before serving. Serve with additional banana slices or a drizzle of maple syrup if desired.

Nutritional Value (Amount per Serving):

Calories: 432; Fat: 22.92; Carb: 63.79; Protein: 13.84

Smashed Avocado and Tomato Toast

Prep Time: 10 Minutes   Cook Time: 5 Minutes   Serves: 2

Ingredients:

- 4 slices of whole-grain bread
- 2 ripe avocados
- Salt and pepper, to taste
- 1 cup cherry tomatoes, halved
- Red pepper flakes (optional)
- Fresh basil leaves, for garnish

Directions:

1. Ensure the Flip Toaster Oven is in toaster mode (flipped up) and heat to 350°F.
2. Place the slices of whole-grain bread in the toaster and toast for 5 minutes or until golden brown.
3. Mash the ripe avocados in a bowl and season with salt and pepper.
4. Spread the mashed avocado evenly on the toasted bread slices.
5. Top with halved cherry tomatoes.
6. Optional: Sprinkle with red pepper flakes and garnish with fresh basil leaves.
7. Serve immediately for a quick and delicious avocado toast.

Nutritional Value (Amount per Serving):

Calories: 560; Fat: 33.12; Carb: 57.56; Protein: 15.78

Maple Pecan Baked French Toast

Prep Time: 15 Minutes   Cook Time: 25 Minutes   Serves: 4-6

Ingredients:

- 1 loaf French bread, sliced
- 4 large eggs
- 1 cup milk
- 1/2 cup pure maple syrup
- 1 teaspoon vanilla extract
- 1/2 cup chopped pecans
- Powdered sugar for dusting

Directions:

1. Use the Bake function and set the temperature to 375°F.
2. Arrange the sliced French bread in a greased baking dish.
3. In a bowl, whisk together eggs, milk, maple syrup, and vanilla extract.
4. Pour the custard over the bread slices, ensuring all are coated. Sprinkle chopped pecans on top.
5. Bake until the custard is set and the top is golden brown, about 20-25 minutes.
6. Dust with powdered sugar before serving.

Nutritional Value (Amount per Serving):

Calories: 243; Fat: 12.48; Carb: 28.99; Protein: 4.97

Veggie-packed Frittata

Prep Time: 15 Minutes   Cook Time: 25 Minutes   Serves: 6

Ingredients:

- 6 large eggs

- 1/2 cup milk
- 1 cup diced bell peppers (assorted colors)
- 1 cup chopped spinach
- 1/2 cup diced cherry tomatoes
- 1/2 cup shredded cheddar cheese
- Salt and pepper to taste

Directions:
1. Flip down the toaster oven for oven mode, set the temperature to 375°F.
2. Saute diced bell peppers, chopped spinach, and cherry tomatoes in a pan until tender.
3. In a bowl, whisk together eggs, milk, salt, and pepper.
4. Mix sautéed vegetables with the egg mixture. Pour the mixture into a greased oven-safe dish.
5. Place the dish in the toaster oven and bake for 20-25 minutes or until the frittata is set and golden on top.
6. Allow the frittata to cool for a few minutes before slicing.
7. Serve warm.

Nutritional Value (Amount per Serving):
Calories: 96; Fat: 6.28; Carb: 4.56; Protein: 5.37

Cinnamon French Toast Sticks

Prep Time: 10 Minutes   Cook Time: 15 Minutes   Serves: 4

Ingredients:
- 8 slices of thick-cut bread
- 2 large eggs
- 1/2 cup milk
- 1 teaspoon vanilla extract
- 1 teaspoon ground cinnamon
- Maple syrup for dipping

Directions:
1. Flip up the toaster oven and set it to the toast function at 400°F.
2. Slice each bread slice into 3-4 sticks.
3. In a bowl, whisk together eggs, milk, vanilla extract, and ground cinnamon.
4. Dip each bread stick into the egg mixture, coating evenly. Place on the toaster oven rack and toast for 8-10 minutes or until golden brown.
5. Arrange the French toast sticks on a plate and serve with maple syrup for dipping.

Nutritional Value (Amount per Serving):
Calories: 161; Fat: 4.59; Carb: 23.29; Protein: 5.88

Smoked Salmon Bagel

Prep Time: 10 Minutes   Cook Time: 5 Minutes   Serves: 2

Ingredients:

- 2 bagels, sliced and toasted
- 4 oz smoked salmon
- 1/2 cup cream cheese
- 1 tablespoon capers
- Red onion slices
- Fresh dill for garnish

Directions:

1. Flip up the toaster oven and set it to the toast function at 400°F.
2. Place bagel halves on the toaster oven rack and toast until golden brown.
3. Spread cream cheese on each bagel half.
4. Top with smoked salmon, capers, red onion slices, and fresh dill.
5. Arrange on a plate and serve immediately.

Nutritional Value (Amount per Serving):

Calories: 518; Fat: 22.93; Carb: 51.64; Protein: 26.6

Blueberry Almond Baked Oatmeal

Prep Time: 15 Minutes   Cook Time: 30 Minutes   Serves: 6

Ingredients:

- 2 cups old-fashioned oats
- 1/2 cup chopped almonds
- 1 teaspoon baking powder
- 1/2 teaspoon cinnamon
- 2 cups milk
- 1/4 cup maple syrup
- 2 eggs
- 1 teaspoon vanilla extract
- 1 cup fresh blueberries

Directions:

1. Flip down the toaster oven for oven mode, set the temperature to 375°F.
2. In a bowl, combine oats, chopped almonds, baking powder, and cinnamon.
3. In another bowl, whisk together milk, maple syrup, eggs, and vanilla extract.
4. Mix the wet and dry ingredients, then fold in fresh blueberries.
5. Pour the mixture into a greased baking dish and bake for 25-30 minutes or until set and golden.
6. Allow to cool slightly before serving.

Nutritional Value (Amount per Serving):

Calories: 245; Fat: 8.28; Carb: 43.87; Protein: 11.29

Banana Walnut Muffins

Prep Time: 15 Minutes   Cook Time: 20 Minutes   Serves: 6

Ingredients:

- 2 cups all-purpose flour
- 1 teaspoon baking soda
- 1/2 teaspoon salt
- 1/2 cup unsalted butter, melted
- 1/2 cup granulated sugar
- 2 large ripe bananas, mashed
- 2 large eggs
- 1 teaspoon vanilla extract
- 1 cup chopped walnuts

Directions:

1. Flip down the toaster oven for oven mode, set the temperature to 375°F.
2. In a bowl, whisk together flour, baking soda, and salt. In another bowl, mix melted butter, sugar, mashed bananas, eggs, and vanilla extract. Combine wet and dry ingredients, then fold in chopped walnuts.
3. Line a muffin tin with paper liners and fill each cup 3/4 full with batter.
4. Bake for 18-20 minutes or until a toothpick inserted into the center comes out clean.
5. Allow muffins to cool in the tin for 5 minutes before transferring to a wire rack.

Nutritional Value (Amount per Serving):

Calories: 425; Fat: 21.04; Carb: 52.58; Protein: 8.34

Breakfast Pizza

Prep Time: 15 Minutes   Cook Time: 10 Minutes   Serves: 4

Ingredients:

- 1 pre-made pizza dough
- 4 large eggs
- 1 cup cooked and crumbled breakfast sausage
- 1 cup shredded mozzarella cheese
- 1/2 cup diced bell peppers (assorted colors)
- Salt and pepper to taste

Directions:

1. Flip down the toaster oven for oven mode, set the temperature to 400°F.
2. Roll out the pizza dough on a floured surface.
3. Transfer the dough to a baking sheet. Sprinkle with mozzarella, add breakfast sausage and diced bell peppers. Create small wells for the eggs.
4. Crack an egg into each well. Bake for 10 minutes or until the crust is golden and eggs are set.
5. Season with salt and pepper. Slice and serve.

Nutritional Value (Amount per Serving):

Calories: 557; Fat: 22.28; Carb: 61.26; Protein: 27.36

Mediterranean Shakshuka

Prep Time: 15 Minutes   Cook Time: 20 Minutes   Serves: 4

Ingredients:

- 1 tablespoon olive oil
- 1 onion, diced
- 2 bell peppers, diced
- 2 cloves garlic, minced
- 1 teaspoon ground cumin
- 1 teaspoon paprika
- 1/2 teaspoon cayenne pepper (optional for heat)
- 1 can (28 oz) crushed tomatoes
- 4-6 large eggs
- Feta cheese and fresh parsley for garnish

Directions:

1. Flip down the toaster oven for oven mode, set the temperature to 375°F.
2. Heat olive oil in an oven-safe skillet. Sauté onions and bell peppers until softened. Add garlic, cumin, paprika, and cayenne pepper (if using).
3. Pour in the crushed tomatoes and simmer for 10 minutes.
4. Make wells in the tomato mixture and crack eggs into each well.
5. Transfer the skillet to the toaster oven and bake for 10-12 minutes or until the eggs are cooked to your liking.
6. Sprinkle with crumbled feta and fresh parsley before serving.

Nutritional Value (Amount per Serving):

Calories: 154; Fat: 11.13; Carb: 8.49; Protein: 6.08

Chapter 2: Chicken and Poultry

Chicken Club Casseroles

Prep Time: 20 Minutes   Cook Time: 35 Minutes   Serves: 5

Ingredients:

- 4 cups uncooked spiral pasta
- 4 cups cubed cooked chicken
- 2 cans (10-3/4 ounces each) condensed cheddar cheese soup, undiluted
- 1 cup crumbled cooked bacon
- 1 cup 2% milk
- 1 cup mayonnaise
- 4 medium tomatoes, seeded and chopped
- 3 cups fresh baby spinach, chopped
- 2 cups shredded Colby-Monterey Jack cheese

Directions:

1. Heat the oven to 375°F. Cook pasta according to package directions.
2. In a large bowl, combine chicken, soup, bacon, milk and mayonnaise. Stir in tomatoes and spinach.
3. Drain pasta; stir into chicken mixture. Transfer to 2 greased 8-in. square baking dishes. Sprinkle with cheese.
4. Cover and bake(one dish at a time) until bubbly and cheese is melted, 35-40 minutes.

Nutritional Value (Amount per Serving):

Calories: 1080; Fat: 79.24; Carb: 50.33; Protein: 45.05

Golden Chicken Cordon Bleu

Prep Time: 12 Minutes   Cook Time: 20 Minutes   Serves: 2

Ingredients:

- 2 boneless skinless chicken breast halves (6 ounces each)
- 2 slices deli ham (3/4 ounce each)
- 2 slices Swiss cheese (3/4 ounce each)
- 1/2 cup all-purpose flour
- 1/4 teaspoon salt
- 1/8 teaspoon paprika
- 1/8 teaspoon pepper
- 1 large egg
- 2 tablespoons 2% milk
- 1/2 cup seasoned bread crumbs
- 1 tablespoon canola oil

- 1 tablespoon butter, melted

Directions:

1. Flatten chicken to 1/4-in. thickness; top each with a slice of ham and cheese.
2. Roll up and tuck in ends; secure with toothpicks.
3. In a shallow bowl, combine the flour, salt, paprika and pepper.
4. In another bowl, whisk egg and milk. Place bread crumbs in a third bowl.
5. Dip chicken in flour mixture, then egg mixture; roll in crumbs.
6. In a small skillet, brown chicken in oil on all sides.
7. Transfer to an 8-in. square baking dish coated with cooking spray.
8. Bake at 350°Funtil a thermometer reads 170°F, for 20-25 minutes.
9. Discard toothpicks; drizzle with butter.

Nutritional Value (Amount per Serving):

Calories: 617; Fat: 28.61; Carb: 33.15; Protein: 53.98

Turkey Meat Loaf

Prep Time: 15 Minutes   Cook Time: 1 Hour   Serves: 10

Ingredients:

- 1 cup quick-cooking oats
- 1 medium onion, chopped
- 1/2 cup shredded carrot
- 1/2 cup fat-free milk
- 1/4 cup egg substitute
- 2 tablespoons ketchup
- 1 teaspoon garlic powder
- 1/4 teaspoon pepper
- 2 pounds lean ground turkey
- 1/4 cup ketchup
- 1/4 cup quick-cooking oats

Directions:

1. Heat the oven to 350°F.
2. Combine first 8 ingredients. Add turkey; mix lightly but thoroughly.
3. Transfer to a loaf pan coated with cooking spray.
4. Mix topping ingredients; spread over loaf.
5. Bake until a thermometer reads 165°F, 60-65 minutes.
6. Let stand 10 minutes before slicing.

Nutritional Value (Amount per Serving):

Calories: 182; Fat: 8.07; Carb: 8.69; Protein: 19.1

Honey Mustard Glazed Turkey Breast

Prep Time: 20 Minutes   Cook Time: 1 Hour   Serves: 8

Ingredients:

- 4 pounds boneless, skinless turkey breast
- 1/2 cup Dijon mustard
- 1/4 cup honey
- 2 tablespoons soy sauce
- 2 cloves garlic, minced
- 1 teaspoon dried thyme
- Salt and pepper to taste

Directions:

1. Heat the Flip Toaster Oven to 400°F in oven mode.
2. Place the turkey breast on a rack in a roasting pan.
3. In a small bowl, whisk together Dijon mustard, honey, soy sauce, minced garlic, dried thyme, salt, and pepper.
4. Brush the turkey breast with the honey mustard glaze, coating it evenly.
5. Roast for 1 hour or until the internal temperature reaches 165°F.
6. Baste the turkey with the glaze every 20 minutes.
7. Let the turkey rest for 10 minutes before slicing.

Nutritional Value (Amount per Serving):

Calories: 451; Fat: 14.16; Carb: 58.82; Protein: 22.09

Crispy Baked Chicken Wings

Prep Time: 10 Minutes   Cook Time: 50 Minutes   Serves: 4

Ingredients:

- 2 pounds chicken wings, split at joints, tips discarded
- 2 tablespoons baking powder
- 1 teaspoon salt
- 1 teaspoon garlic powder
- 1 teaspoon smoked paprika
- 1/2 teaspoon black pepper
- Your favorite wing sauce for serving

Directions:

1. Heat the Flip Toaster Oven to 400°F in oven mode.
2. In a large bowl, toss the wings with baking powder, salt, garlic powder, smoked paprika, and black pepper until evenly coated.
3. Place the wings on the oven rack in a single layer, skin side up.
4. Bake for 40-45 minutes, turning halfway through, until wings are golden and crispy.
5. Toss the wings in your favorite sauce before serving.

Nutritional Value (Amount per Serving):

Calories: 300; Fat: 8.16; Carb: 5.11; Protein: 50.19

Coconut Curry Chicken Drumsticks

Prep Time: 20 Minutes   Cook Time: 45 Minutes   Serves: 6

Ingredients:

- 12 chicken drumsticks
- 1 can (14 oz) coconut milk
- 2 tablespoons red curry paste
- 1 tablespoon soy sauce
- 1 tablespoon brown sugar
- 1 tablespoon lime juice
- Fresh cilantro for garnish

Directions:

1. Heat the Toaster Oven to 400°F in oven mode.
2. In a bowl, mix coconut milk, red curry paste, soy sauce, brown sugar, and lime juice.
3. Place chicken drumsticks in a baking dish and pour the coconut curry mixture over them.
4. Bake for 40-45 minutes, basting occasionally, until the chicken is cooked through.
5. Garnish with fresh cilantro before serving.

Nutritional Value (Amount per Serving):

Calories: 589; Fat: 40.49; Carb: 6.69; Protein: 49.12

Pesto Stuffed Chicken Breasts

Prep Time: 25 Minutes   Cook Time: 30 Minutes   Serves: 4

Ingredients:

- 4 boneless, skinless chicken breasts
- 1/2 cup pesto sauce
- 1 cup cherry tomatoes, halved
- 1 cup fresh mozzarella balls, halved
- Salt and pepper to taste
- Toothpicks

Directions:

1. Heat the Toaster Oven to 400°F in oven mode.
2. Butterfly the chicken breasts and spread pesto inside.
3. Place halved cherry tomatoes and mozzarella on one side of the chicken.
4. Fold the chicken over the filling and secure with toothpicks.
5. Season the stuffed chicken with salt and pepper.
6. Bake for 30 minutes or until the chicken is cooked through.

Nutritional Value (Amount per Serving):

Calories: 621; Fat: 31.37; Carb: 58.29; Protein: 26.81

Crispy Parmesan Baked Chicken Tenders

Prep Time: 15 Minutes   Cook Time: 20 Minutes   Serves: 4

Ingredients:

- 1 pound chicken tenders
- 1 cup breadcrumbs
- 1/2 cup grated Parmesan cheese
- 1 teaspoon garlic powder
- 1 teaspoon dried oregano
- Salt and pepper to taste
- 2 eggs, beaten

Directions:

1. Heat the Toaster Oven to 400°F in oven mode.
2. In a bowl, mix breadcrumbs, Parmesan cheese, garlic powder, oregano, salt, and pepper.
3. Dip each chicken tender into beaten eggs, then coat with the breadcrumb mixture.
4. Place the tenders on a baking sheet.
5. Bake for 20 minutes or until the chicken is cooked through and crispy.

Nutritional Value (Amount per Serving):

Calories: 411; Fat: 22.96; Carb: 23.96; Protein: 26.95

Apricot Glazed Chicken Drumettes

Prep Time: 15 Minutes   Cook Time: 30 Minutes   Serves: 6

Ingredients:

- 2 pounds chicken drumettes
- 1/2 cup apricot preserves
- 2 tablespoons Dijon mustard
- 1 tablespoon soy sauce
- 1 teaspoon minced ginger
- Sesame seeds for garnish

Directions:

1. Heat the Toaster Oven to 400°F in oven mode.
2. In a saucepan, heat apricot preserves, Dijon mustard, soy sauce, and minced ginger until well combined.
3. Place chicken drumettes on a baking sheet and brush with the apricot glaze.
4. Bake for 25-30 minutes, turning and basting halfway through.
5. Garnish with sesame seeds before serving.

Nutritional Value (Amount per Serving):

Calories: 208; Fat: 5.07; Carb: 7.86; Protein: 31.59

Spinach and Feta Stuffed Chicken Breasts

Prep Time: 25 Minutes   Cook Time: 35 Minutes   Serves: 4

Ingredients:

- 4 boneless, skinless chicken breasts
- 2 cups fresh spinach, chopped
- 1/2 cup crumbled feta cheese
- 2 cloves garlic, minced
- 1 teaspoon dried oregano
- Salt and pepper to taste
- Toothpicks

Directions:

1. Heat the Toaster Oven to 400°F in oven mode.
2. In a bowl, mix chopped spinach, feta cheese, minced garlic, oregano, salt, and pepper.
3. Butterfly the chicken breasts and stuff with the spinach and feta mixture.
4. Secure with toothpicks.
5. Bake for 30-35 minutes or until the chicken is cooked through.

Nutritional Value (Amount per Serving):

Calories: 495; Fat: 18.31; Carb: 55.27; Protein: 26.61

Mediterranean Chicken and Vegetable Skewers

Prep Time: 30 Minutes   Cook Time: 25 Minutes   Serves: 4

Ingredients:

- 1 pound boneless, skinless chicken thighs, cut into cubes
- 1 zucchini, sliced
- 1 red bell pepper, cut into chunks
- 1 red onion, cut into wedges
- 1/4 cup olive oil
- 2 tablespoons balsamic vinegar
- 1 teaspoon dried oregano
- Salt and pepper to taste
- Wooden skewers, soaked in water

Directions:

1. Heat the Toaster Oven to 400°F in oven mode.
2. In a bowl, combine chicken, zucchini, red bell pepper, red onion, olive oil, balsamic vinegar, oregano, salt, and pepper.
3. Thread the chicken and vegetables onto the soaked skewers.
4. Bake for 20-25 minutes or until the chicken is cooked through.

Nutritional Value (Amount per Serving):

Calories: 345; Fat: 20.05; Carb: 30.01; Protein: 11.4

Maple Mustard Glazed Chicken Thighs

Prep Time: 15 Minutes   Cook Time: 40 Minutes   Serves: 4

Ingredients:

- 8 bone-in, skin-on chicken thighs
- 1/3 cup maple syrup
- 2 tablespoons Dijon mustard
- 1 tablespoon soy sauce
- 1 tablespoon apple cider vinegar
- 1 teaspoon garlic powder
- Salt and pepper to taste

Directions:

1. Heat the Flip Toaster Oven to 400°F in oven mode.
2. Season chicken thighs with salt and pepper.
3. In a bowl, whisk together maple syrup, Dijon mustard, soy sauce, apple cider vinegar, and garlic powder.
4. Brush the chicken thighs with the maple mustard glaze.
5. Bake for 35-40 minutes or until the chicken is golden and reaches an internal temperature of 165°F.

Nutritional Value (Amount per Serving):

Calories: 1091; Fat: 101.34; Carb: 22.73; Protein: 22.67

Caprese Stuffed Chicken Roll-Ups

Prep Time: 20 Minutes   Cook Time: 25 Minutes   Serves: 4

Ingredients:

- 4 boneless, skinless chicken breasts
- 1 cup cherry tomatoes, halved
- 1 cup fresh mozzarella balls, halved
- 1/4 cup fresh basil, chopped
- 2 tablespoons balsamic glaze
- Salt and pepper to taste
- Toothpicks

Directions:

1. Heat the Flip Toaster Oven to 400°F in oven mode.
2. Flatten each chicken breast, season with salt and pepper.
3. Place cherry tomatoes, mozzarella, and fresh basil on each chicken breast.
4. Roll up the chicken and secure with toothpicks.
5. Bake for 20-25 minutes or until the chicken is cooked through.
6. Drizzle with balsamic glaze before serving.

Nutritional Value (Amount per Serving):

Calories: 466; Fat: 14.47; Carb: 59.39; Protein: 24.45

Honey Soy Glazed Chicken Thighs

Prep Time: 15 Minutes   Cook Time: 40 Minutes   Serves: 4

Ingredients:

- 8 bone-in, skin-on chicken thighs
- 1/4 cup honey
- 3 tablespoons soy sauce
- 2 tablespoons olive oil
- 1 tablespoon Dijon mustard
- 2 cloves garlic, minced
- 1 teaspoon dried thyme
- Salt and pepper to taste

Directions:

1. Heat the Toaster Oven to 400°F in oven mode.
2. In a bowl, whisk together honey, soy sauce, olive oil, Dijon mustard, minced garlic, thyme, salt, and pepper.
3. Coat the chicken thighs with the honey soy glaze.
4. Place the thighs on a baking sheet.
5. Bake for 35-40 minutes or until the chicken is cooked through.

Nutritional Value (Amount per Serving):

Calories: 1166; Fat: 109.39; Carb: 24.07; Protein: 23.12

Crispy Baked Parmesan Chicken Breasts

Prep Time: 15 Minutes   Cook Time: 30 Minutes   Serves: 4

Ingredients:

- 4 boneless, skinless chicken breasts
- 1 cup breadcrumbs
- 1/2 cup grated Parmesan cheese
- 1 teaspoon garlic powder
- 1 teaspoon dried basil
- Salt and pepper to taste
- 2 eggs, beaten

Directions:

1. Heat the Toaster Oven to 400°F in oven mode.
2. In a bowl, mix breadcrumbs, Parmesan cheese, garlic powder, dried basil, salt, and pepper.
3. Dip each chicken breast into beaten eggs, then coat with the breadcrumb mixture.
4. Place the breasts on a baking sheet.
5. Bake for 25-30 minutes or until the chicken is cooked through and golden.

Nutritional Value (Amount per Serving):

Calories: 560; Fat: 22.56; Carb: 56.18; Protein: 31.6

Pomegranate Glazed Turkey Meatballs

Prep Time: 20 Minutes   Cook Time: 25 Minutes   Serves: 6

Ingredients:
- 1.5 pounds ground turkey
- 1/2 cup breadcrumbs
- 1/4 cup grated onion
- 2 cloves garlic, minced
- 1 egg
- 1/2 cup pomegranate juice
- 2 tablespoons soy sauce
- 2 tablespoons honey
- 1 teaspoon ground ginger
- Sesame seeds for garnish

Directions:
1. Heat the Toaster Oven to 400°F in oven mode.
2. In a bowl, combine ground turkey, breadcrumbs, grated onion, minced garlic, and egg.
3. Form the mixture into meatballs and place them on a baking sheet.
4. In a saucepan, simmer pomegranate juice, soy sauce, honey, and ground ginger until it thickens.
5. Brush the meatballs with the pomegranate glaze and bake for 20-25 minutes.
6. Garnish with sesame seeds before serving.

Nutritional Value (Amount per Serving):

Calories: 245; Fat: 11.61; Carb: 11.03; Protein: 24.46

Cranberry Pecan Stuffed Chicken Thighs

Prep Time: 25 Minutes   Cook Time: 35 Minutes   Serves: 4

Ingredients:
- 8 bone-in, skin-on chicken thighs
- 1/2 cup dried cranberries, chopped
- 1/2 cup pecans, chopped
- 1/4 cup breadcrumbs
- 2 tablespoons fresh sage, chopped
- Salt and pepper to taste
- Cooking twine

Directions:
1. Heat the Toaster Oven to 400°F in oven mode.
2. In a bowl, mix dried cranberries, pecans, breadcrumbs, fresh sage, salt, and pepper.
3. Stuff each chicken thigh with the cranberry pecan mixture and secure with cooking twine.
4. Place the thighs on a baking sheet.
5. Bake for 30-35 minutes or until the chicken is cooked through.

Nutritional Value (Amount per Serving):

Calories: 1109; Fat: 109.41; Carb: 9.72; Protein: 23.24

Chapter 3: Beef, Pork and Lamb

Spinach Beef Pie

Prep Time: 25 Minutes   Cook Time: 40 Minutes   Serves: 8

Ingredients:

- 1 cup all-purpose flour
- 1/3 cup old-fashioned oats
- 7 tablespoons cold butter
- 2 to 3 tablespoons cold water
- 1 pound ground beef
- 1 medium onion, chopped
- 1 medium green pepper, chopped
- 1 garlic clove, minced
- 1/4 cup ketchup
- 1 teaspoon salt
- 1 teaspoon dried oregano
- 1/2 teaspoon dried basil
- 1/2 teaspoon dried marjoram
- 1/4 teaspoon pepper
- 1 package (10 ounces) frozen chopped spinach, thawed and squeezed dry
- 3 large eggs, lightly beaten
- 2 cups shredded cheddar cheese, divided
- 1 large tomato, seeded and diced

Directions:

1. In a large bowl, combine flour and oats; cut in the butter until crumbly. Gradually add water, tossing with a fork until dough forms a ball.
2. Roll out dough to fit a pie plate. Transfer to plate; trim and flute edges.
3. Heat the oven to 400°F. In a large skillet, cook the beef, onion, green pepper and garlic over medium heat until meat is no longer pink; drain.
4. Stir in the ketchup and seasonings. Fold in the spinach; cool slightly. Stir in the eggs and 1 cup cheese until combined; spoon into crust.
5. Bake until the center is set, 25-30 minutes. Sprinkle with tomato and remaining cheese around edge of pie. Bake until cheese is melted, 5-10 minutes longer. Let stand for 5-10 minutes before cutting.

Nutritional Value (Amount per Serving):

Calories: 426; Fat: 25.44; Carb: 25.92; Protein: 25.33

Italian-Style Baked Meatballs

Prep Time: 20 Minutes   Cook Time: 30 Minutes   Serves: 6-8

Ingredients:

- 1.5 lbs ground beef
- 1 cup breadcrumbs
- 1/2 cup grated Parmesan cheese
- 1/4 cup fresh parsley, chopped
- 2 cloves garlic, minced
- 1 egg
- 2 cups marinara sauce

Directions:

1. Heat the toaster oven to 375°F in bake mode.

2. In a large bowl, mix ground beef, breadcrumbs, Parmesan cheese, parsley, minced garlic, and egg until well combined.
3. Form meatballs and place them on a baking sheet.
4. Bake in bake mode for 20-25 minutes until the meatballs are browned and cooked through.
5. Switch to broil mode for the last 5 minutes for a golden crust.
6. Heat the marinara sauce in a saucepan.
7. Serve the meatballs with the warm marinara sauce.

Nutritional Value (Amount per Serving):

Calories: 335; Fat: 20.19; Carb: 7.48; Protein: 29.01

Herb-Crusted Lamb Chops

Prep Time: 10 Minutes   Cook Time: 25 Minutes   Serves: 4

Ingredients:

- 8 lamb chops
- 2 tablespoons fresh parsley, chopped
- 1 tablespoon fresh thyme, chopped
- 2 cloves garlic, minced
- 2 tablespoons olive oil
- Salt and pepper to taste

Directions:

1. Heat the toaster oven to 400°F in bake mode.
2. In a bowl, mix chopped parsley, thyme, minced garlic, olive oil, salt, and pepper to create a herb crust.
3. Press the herb crust onto both sides of each lamb chop.
4. Place the lamb chops on a baking sheet and bake in bake mode for 20-25 minutes.
5. Switch to broil mode for the last 5 minutes to achieve a golden crust.
6. Allow the lamb chops to rest for 5 minutes before serving.

Nutritional Value (Amount per Serving):

Calories: 551; Fat: 30.21; Carb: 1.83; Protein: 68.38

Oven-Baked BBQ Pork Ribs

Prep Time: 15 Minutes   Cook Time: 2 Hours   Serves: 6-8

Ingredients:

- 3 lbs pork ribs
- 1 cup barbecue sauce
- 2 tablespoons brown sugar
- 1 tablespoon paprika
- 1 teaspoon garlic powder

Directions:

1. Heat the toaster oven to 375°F in bake mode.

2. Mix barbecue sauce, brown sugar, paprika, and garlic powder in a bowl.
3. Place the pork ribs on a baking sheet, and brush both sides with the sauce mixture.
4. Cover the ribs with aluminum foil and bake for 1.5 hours.
5. Remove the foil, brush with more sauce, and switch to broil mode for an additional 15 minutes for a caramelized finish.
6. Allow the ribs to rest for 10 minutes before serving.

Nutritional Value (Amount per Serving):

Calories: 350; Fat: 11.35; Carb: 18.4; Protein: 40.9

Honey Glazed Baked Ham

Prep Time: 15 Minutes   Cook Time: 2 Hours   Serves: 6-8

Ingredients:

- 1 bone-in ham (about 5 lbs)
- 1 cup honey
- 1/2 cup Dijon mustard
- 1/4 cup brown sugar
- 1 teaspoon ground cloves

Directions:

1. Heat the toaster oven to 350°F in bake mode.
2. Score the surface of the ham in a diamond pattern.
3. In a bowl, mix honey, Dijon mustard, brown sugar, and ground cloves to create the glaze.
4. Place the ham in a roasting pan, and generously brush the glaze over the entire surface.
5. Cover the ham with aluminum foil and bake for 1.5 hours.
6. Remove the foil, baste with additional glaze, and switch to broil mode for 10 minutes to caramelize the top.
7. Allow the ham to rest for 10 minutes before carving.

Nutritional Value (Amount per Serving):

Calories: 524; Fat: 11.92; Carb: 51.79; Protein: 56.37

French Onion Beef Sliders

Prep Time: 15 Minutes   Cook Time: 25 Minutes   Serves: 4-6

Ingredients:

- 1 lb ground beef
- 1 packet French onion soup mix
- 1 cup Gruyère cheese, shredded
- Slider buns
- Salt and pepper to taste

Directions:

1. Heat the toaster oven to 375°F in bake mode.
2. In a bowl, mix ground beef and French onion soup mix. Form small patties.
3. Place the patties on a baking sheet, season with salt and pepper, and bake for 20 minutes.
4. Top each patty with Gruyère cheese and broil for an additional 5 minutes until cheese is melted and bubbly.
5. Serve the sliders on toasted buns.

Nutritional Value (Amount per Serving):

Calories: 389; Fat: 23.99; Carb: 12.97; Protein: 18.66

Pork and Apple Stuffed Acorn Squash

Prep Time: 20 Minutes   Cook Time: 45 Minutes   Serves: 4

Ingredients:

- 2 acorn squash, halved and seeds removed
- 1 lb ground pork
- 2 apples, diced
- 1/2 cup breadcrumbs
- 1 teaspoon sage, chopped
- Salt and pepper to taste

Directions:

1. Heat the toaster oven to 375°F in bake mode.
2. Place the acorn squash halves on a baking sheet.
3. In a skillet, cook ground pork until browned. Add diced apples, breadcrumbs, sage, salt, and pepper. Mix well.
4. Fill each acorn squash half with the pork and apple mixture.
5. Bake for 40 minutes, then switch to broil for the last 5 minutes for a golden top.

Nutritional Value (Amount per Serving):

Calories: 475; Fat: 23.97; Carb: 36.19; Protein: 31.34

Lamb and Vegetable Kebabs

Prep Time: 20 Minutes   Cook Time: 15 Minutes   Serves: 4

Ingredients:

- 1 lb lamb, cut into cubes
- 1 bell pepper, cut into chunks

- 1 red onion, cut into wedges
- 1 zucchini, sliced
- 2 tablespoons olive oil
- 1 teaspoon cumin
- 1 teaspoon paprika
- Salt and pepper to taste

Directions:

1. Heat the toaster oven to 400°F in bake mode.
2. In a bowl, toss lamb, bell pepper, red onion, and zucchini with olive oil, cumin, paprika, salt, and pepper.
3. Thread the mixture onto skewers and place on a baking sheet.
4. Bake for 12-15 minutes, turning halfway through.
5. For the last 3 minutes, switch to broil for a nicely charred finish.

Nutritional Value (Amount per Serving):

Calories: 374; Fat: 26.1; Carb: 5.33; Protein: 28.81

Sweet and Sour Pineapple Pork

Prep Time: 15 Minutes   Cook Time: 25 Minutes   Serves: 4

Ingredients:

- 1 lb pork tenderloin, sliced
- 1 cup pineapple chunks
- 1 bell pepper, sliced
- 1/2 cup sweet and sour sauce
- 2 tablespoons soy sauce
- 1 tablespoon cornstarch

Directions:

1. Preheat the toaster oven to 375°F in bake mode.
2. In a bowl, mix pork slices, pineapple chunks, bell pepper, sweet and sour sauce, soy sauce, and cornstarch.
3. Transfer the mixture to a baking dish and bake for 25 minutes.
4. Switch to broil for the last 5 minutes to caramelize the top.
5. Serve over rice.

Nutritional Value (Amount per Serving):

Calories: 303; Fat: 5.51; Carb: 31.85; Protein: 30.81

Herb-Crusted Beef Baguette Sandwich

Prep Time: 15 Minutes   Cook Time: 20 Minutes   Serves: 4

Ingredients:

- 1 lb beef sirloin, thinly sliced
- 1 baguette, sliced
- 2 tablespoons Dijon mustard
- 1 tablespoon horseradish
- 1 cup arugula
- 1 tablespoon olive oil
- Fresh thyme leaves for garnish

Directions:

1. Heat the toaster oven to 400°F in bake mode.
2. Mix Dijon mustard and horseradish in a small bowl.
3. Brush each baguette slice with the mustard-horseradish mixture.
4. Arrange the beef slices on top and bake for 10 minutes.
5. In the last 2 minutes, switch to broil to toast the baguette.
6. Toss arugula with olive oil and place it on top of the beef.
7. Garnish with fresh thyme leaves before serving.

Nutritional Value (Amount per Serving):

Calories: 434; Fat: 31.74; Carb: 2.8; Protein: 33.67

Mango-Glazed Pork Chops

Prep Time: 15 Minutes   Cook Time: 20 Minutes   Serves: 4

Ingredients:

- 4 pork chops
- 1 mango, peeled and pureed
- 1/4 cup soy sauce
- 2 tablespoons honey
- 1 tablespoon ginger, minced

Directions:

1. Heat the toaster oven to 375°F in bake mode.
2. In a bowl, mix mango puree, soy sauce, honey, and minced ginger to create the glaze.
3. Place pork chops in a baking dish and brush with the mango glaze.
4. Bake for 20 minutes, then switch to broil for the last 5 minutes for a caramelized finish.
5. Serve with additional glaze on the side.

Nutritional Value (Amount per Serving):

Calories: 432; Fat: 20.42; Carb: 19.06; Protein: 41.74

Stuffed Bell Peppers with Ground Beef

Prep Time: 25 Minutes   Cook Time: 30 Minutes   Serves: 4

Ingredients:

- 4 bell peppers, halved and seeds removed
- 1 lb ground beef
- 1 cup cooked rice
- 1 cup tomato sauce
- 1 teaspoon Italian seasoning
- Salt and pepper to taste
- Shredded mozzarella cheese for topping

Directions:

1. Heat the toaster oven to 375°F in bake mode.
2. Brown ground beef in a skillet and mix with cooked rice, tomato sauce, Italian seasoning, salt, and pepper.
3. Stuff each bell pepper half with the beef mixture.
4. Place stuffed peppers in a baking dish and bake for 25 minutes.
5. Sprinkle shredded mozzarella cheese on top and broil for the last 5 minutes until bubbly.

Nutritional Value (Amount per Serving):

Calories: 487; Fat: 25.57; Carb: 34.17; Protein: 35.99

Pork and Veggie Stir-Fry

Prep Time: 15 Minutes   Cook Time: 20 Minutes   Serves: 4

Ingredients:

- 1 lb pork tenderloin, sliced
- 2 cups broccoli florets
- 1 bell pepper, sliced
- 1 carrot, julienned
- 3 tablespoons soy sauce
- 1 tablespoon hoisin sauce
- 1 tablespoon sesame oil

Directions:

1. Heat the toaster oven to 400°F in bake mode.
2. Toss pork slices, broccoli, bell pepper, and carrot with soy sauce, hoisin sauce, and sesame oil.
3. Spread the mixture on a baking sheet and bake for 15 minutes.
4. Switch to broil for the last 5 minutes to caramelize the edges.
5. Serve over rice or noodles.

Nutritional Value (Amount per Serving):

Calories: 251; Fat: 9.84; Carb: 7.83; Protein: 31.66

Mint and Garlic Marinated Lamb Kebabs

Prep Time: 20 Minutes   Cook Time: 15 Minutes   Serves: 4

Ingredients:

- 1 lb lamb, cut into cubes
- 2 tablespoons fresh mint, chopped
- 2 cloves garlic, minced
- 1/4 cup olive oil
- 1 teaspoon cumin
- Salt and pepper to taste

Directions:

1. Heat the toaster oven to 400°F in bake mode.

2. In a bowl, mix lamb cubes, chopped mint, minced garlic, olive oil, cumin, salt, and pepper.
3. Marinate for 15 minutes.
4. Thread the lamb onto skewers and place on a baking sheet.
5. Broil for 12-15 minutes, turning halfway through.

Nutritional Value (Amount per Serving):

Calories: 582; Fat: 41.4; Carb: 1.79; Protein: 48.32

Cuban-Style Mojo Pork Skewers

Prep Time: 20 Minutes   Cook Time: 15 Minutes   Serves: 4

Ingredients:

- 1 lb pork tenderloin, cut into cubes
- 1/4 cup orange juice
- 2 tablespoons lime juice
- 2 cloves garlic, minced
- 1 teaspoon cumin
- 1 teaspoon oregano
- Pineapple chunks for skewering

Directions:

1. Heat the toaster oven to 400°F in bake mode.
2. In a bowl, mix orange juice, lime juice, minced garlic, cumin, and oregano.
3. Thread pork cubes and pineapple chunks onto skewers.
4. Place skewers on a baking sheet and brush with the mojo marinade.
5. Bake for 12-15 minutes, turning once.

Nutritional Value (Amount per Serving):

Calories: 214; Fat: 4.19; Carb: 13.11; Protein: 30.29

Moroccan Lamb Meatball Tagine

Prep Time: 25 Minutes   Cook Time: 30 Minutes   Serves: 4

Ingredients:

- 1 lb ground lamb
- 1/2 cup breadcrumbs
- 1/4 cup chopped cilantro
- 1 teaspoon ground cumin
- 1 teaspoon ground coriander
- 1 can diced tomatoes
- 1/2 cup chicken broth
- 1/4 cup raisins
- Couscous for serving

Directions:

1. Heat the toaster oven to 375°F in bake mode.
2. In a bowl, mix ground lamb, breadcrumbs, chopped cilantro, cumin, and coriander. Form into meatballs.

3. Place the meatballs in a baking dish.
4. In a separate bowl, mix diced tomatoes, chicken broth, and raisins. Pour over the meatballs.
5. Bake for 25-30 minutes until the meatballs are cooked through.
6. Serve over cooked couscous.

Nutritional Value (Amount per Serving):

Calories: 284; Fat: 16.4; Carb: 3.82; Protein: 30.3

Chipotle Pork Enchiladas

Prep Time: 25 Minutes   Cook Time: 20 Minutes   Serves: 4

Ingredients:

- 1 lb pork shoulder, cooked and shredded
- 1 can black beans, drained and rinsed
- 1 cup corn kernels
- 1 cup shredded Monterey Jack cheese
- 1 can enchilada sauce
- 1 tablespoon chipotle peppers in adobo sauce, minced
- Corn tortillas

Directions:

1. Heat the toaster oven to 375°F in bake mode.
2. In a bowl, mix shredded pork, black beans, corn, half of the cheese, and minced chipotle peppers.
3. Warm corn tortillas in the toaster oven.
4. Fill each tortilla with the pork mixture, roll, and place seam-side down in a baking dish.
5. Pour enchilada sauce over the top and sprinkle with the remaining cheese.
6. Bake for 15-20 minutes until bubbly.

Nutritional Value (Amount per Serving):

Calories: 688; Fat: 34.62; Carb: 48.02; Protein: 46.94

Balsamic-Glazed Beef Skewers

Prep Time: 20 Minutes   Cook Time: 15 Minutes   Serves: 4

Ingredients:

- 1 lb beef sirloin, cut into cubes
- 1/4 cup balsamic vinegar
- 2 tablespoons olive oil
- 1 tablespoon Dijon mustard
- 1 teaspoon dried thyme
- Cherry tomatoes for skewering

Directions:

1. Heat the toaster oven to 400°F in bake mode.
2. In a bowl, mix balsamic vinegar, olive oil, Dijon mustard, and dried thyme.
3. Thread beef cubes and cherry tomatoes onto skewers.
4. Place skewers on a baking sheet and brush with the balsamic mixture.
5. Bake for 12-15 minutes, turning once.

Nutritional Value (Amount per Serving):

Calories: 292; Fat: 19.51; Carb: 3.32; Protein: 23.71

Lemon-Honey Glazed Lamb Ribs

Prep Time: 15 Minutes   Cook Time: 1 Hour 30 Minutes   Serves: 4

Ingredients:

- 2 lbs lamb ribs
- Zest and juice of 2 lemons
- 1/4 cup honey
- 2 tablespoons soy sauce
- 1 teaspoon garlic powder

Directions:

1. Heat the toaster oven to 375°F in bake mode.
2. In a bowl, mix lemon zest, lemon juice, honey, soy sauce, and garlic powder to create the glaze.
3. Place lamb ribs on a baking sheet and brush with the glaze.
4. Cover with aluminum foil and bake for 1 hour.
5. Uncover, brush with more glaze, and switch to broil for an additional 30 minutes, turning halfway.

Nutritional Value (Amount per Serving):

Calories: 479; Fat: 22.44; Carb: 21.67; Protein: 46.16

Pork and Apple Quesadillas

Prep Time: 20 Minutes   Cook Time: 15 Minutes   Serves: 4

Ingredients:

- 1 lb pork loin, cooked and shredded
- 2 apples, thinly sliced
- 1 cup cheddar cheese, shredded
- 1/4 cup caramelized onions
- Flour tortillas
- Sour cream for serving

Directions:

1. Heat the toaster oven to 375°F in bake mode.
2. Lay out tortillas and evenly distribute shredded pork, apple slices, cheddar cheese, and caramelized onions on half of each tortilla.

3. Fold the tortillas in half and place on a baking sheet.
4. Bake for 10-12 minutes until the cheese is melted.
5. Slice into wedges and serve with a dollop of sour cream.

Nutritional Value (Amount per Serving):

Calories: 397; Fat: 17.54; Carb: 23.55; Protein: 35.54

Spicy BBQ Beef Tacos

Prep Time: 20 Minutes   Cook Time: 15 Minutes   Serves: 4

Ingredients:

- 1 lb beef sirloin, thinly sliced
- 1/2 cup barbecue sauce
- 1 tablespoon hot sauce
- 1 teaspoon chili powder
- 1 teaspoon cumin
- Corn tortillas
- Shredded lettuce and diced tomatoes for topping

Directions:

1. Heat the toaster oven to 375°F in bake mode.
2. In a bowl, mix beef slices with barbecue sauce, hot sauce, chili powder, and cumin.
3. Spread the beef mixture on a baking sheet and bake for 15 minutes.
4. Warm corn tortillas in the toaster oven.
5. Fill each tortilla with spicy BBQ beef and top with shredded lettuce and diced tomatoes.

Nutritional Value (Amount per Serving):

Calories: 386; Fat: 14.44; Carb: 36.79; Protein: 26.78

Chapter 4: Fish and Seafood

Lemon Herb Baked Salmon

Prep Time: 15 Minutes   Cook Time: 25 Minutes   Serves: 4

Ingredients:

- 4 salmon fillets
- 2 tablespoons olive oil
- 2 tablespoons fresh lemon juice
- 1 teaspoon minced garlic
- 1 teaspoon dried oregano
- Salt and pepper to taste
- Lemon slices for garnish
- Fresh parsley for garnish

Directions:

1. Heat your Flip Toaster Oven to 400°F in oven mode.
2. Place the salmon fillets on a baking sheet lined with parchment paper.
3. In a small bowl, mix olive oil, lemon juice, minced garlic, oregano, salt, and pepper.
4. Brush the salmon fillets with the prepared mixture, ensuring an even coating.
5. Bake in the oven for 20-25 minutes or until the salmon flakes easily with a fork.
6. Garnish with lemon slices and fresh parsley before serving.

Nutritional Value (Amount per Serving):

Calories: 160; Fat: 10.96; Carb: 3.27; Protein: 12.27

Garlic Butter Shrimp Skewers

Prep Time: 10 Minutes   Cook Time: 15 Minutes   Serves: 4

Ingredients:

- 1 pound large shrimp, peeled and deveined
- 4 tablespoons melted butter
- 3 cloves garlic, minced
- 1 tablespoon chopped fresh parsley
- 1 teaspoon lemon zest
- Salt and pepper to taste
- Wooden skewers, soaked in water

Directions:

1. Heat your Flip Toaster Oven to 400°F in bake mode.
2. In a bowl, mix melted butter, minced garlic, chopped parsley, lemon zest, salt, and pepper.
3. Thread shrimp onto the soaked skewers and place them on a baking sheet.
4. Brush the shrimp with the garlic butter mixture.
5. Bake for 10-12 minutes, turning once, until shrimp are pink and opaque.

6. Switch to broil mode for the last 2-3 minutes to achieve a slightly charred finish.
7. Serve immediately with additional lemon wedges.

Nutritional Value (Amount per Serving):

Calories: 124; Fat: 11.74; Carb: 4.41; Protein: 1.19

Cajun Baked Catfish

Prep Time: 15 Minutes   Cook Time: 20 Minutes   Serves: 4

Ingredients:

- 4 catfish fillets
- 2 tablespoons Cajun seasoning
- 1/4 cup mayonnaise
- 1 tablespoon Dijon mustard
- 1 tablespoon lemon juice
- 1 cup breadcrumbs
- Lemon wedges for serving

Directions:

1. Heat your Flip Toaster Oven to 400°F in bake mode.
2. Rub Cajun seasoning evenly over each catfish fillet.
3. In a bowl, mix mayonnaise, Dijon mustard, and lemon juice.
4. Dip each fillet into the mayo mixture, then coat with breadcrumbs.
5. Place the fillets on a baking sheet and bake for 15-20 minutes or until fish is cooked through.
6. Serve with lemon wedges on the side.

Nutritional Value (Amount per Serving):

Calories: 219; Fat: 9.42; Carb: 4.26; Protein: 27.33

Lemon Dill Baked Whole Branzino

Prep Time: 20 Minutes   Cook Time: 30 Minutes   Serves: 2-4

Ingredients:

- 2 whole branzino, gutted and scaled
- 2 tablespoons olive oil
- 2 tablespoons fresh lemon juice
- 1 tablespoon chopped fresh dill
- 2 cloves garlic, thinly sliced
- Salt and pepper to taste
- Lemon slices for garnish

Directions:

1. Heat your Flip Toaster Oven to 400°F in oven mode.
2. Rinse and pat dry the branzino, then make three diagonal cuts on each side.
3. Mix olive oil, lemon juice, chopped dill, sliced garlic, salt, and pepper in a

bowl.
4. Rub the branzino inside and out with the prepared mixture.
5. Place the fish on a baking sheet and bake for 25-30 minutes until the skin is crispy and the flesh is flaky.
6. Garnish with lemon slices before serving.

Nutritional Value (Amount per Serving):

Calories: 212; Fat: 15.32; Carb: 13.81; Protein: 6.59

Crispy Baked Fish Tacos

Prep Time: 20 Minutes   Cook Time: 15 Minutes   Serves: 4

Ingredients:

- 1 pound white fish fillets (cod or tilapia)
- 1 cup breadcrumbs
- 1 teaspoon smoked paprika
- 1 teaspoon garlic powder
- 1/2 cup plain Greek yogurt
- 1 tablespoon lime juice
- 1 cup shredded cabbage
- 8 small flour tortillas
- Salsa and lime wedges for serving

Directions:

1. Heat your Flip Toaster Oven to 400°F in oven mode.
2. In a shallow bowl, mix breadcrumbs, smoked paprika, and garlic powder.
3. Coat each fish fillet in the breadcrumb mixture and place on a baking sheet.
4. Bake for 12-15 minutes or until the fish is golden and crispy.
5. In a small bowl, combine Greek yogurt and lime juice for the sauce.
6. Assemble tacos with shredded cabbage, baked fish, and a drizzle of lime yogurt sauce.
7. Serve with salsa and lime wedges.

Nutritional Value (Amount per Serving):

Calories: 1341; Fat: 119.63; Carb: 55.27; Protein: 10.12

Pesto Baked Tilapia

Prep Time: 15 Minutes   Cook Time: 25 Minutes   Serves: 4

Ingredients:

- 4 tilapia fillets
- 1/2 cup pesto sauce
- 1 cup cherry tomatoes, halved
- 1/4 cup grated Parmesan cheese
- Salt and pepper to taste
- Fresh basil for garnish

Directions:

1. Heat your Toaster Oven to 400°F in bake mode.

2. Place tilapia fillets on a baking sheet.
3. Spread a layer of pesto sauce over each fillet.
4. Arrange halved cherry tomatoes on top and sprinkle with Parmesan cheese.
5. Season with salt and pepper.
6. Bake for 15 minutes, then switch to broil mode for an additional 3-5 minutes until the top is golden.
7. Garnish with fresh basil before serving.

Nutritional Value (Amount per Serving):

Calories: 311; Fat: 20.8; Carb: 3.69; Protein: 28.56

Teriyaki Glazed Salmon Skewers

Prep Time: 20 Minutes   Cook Time: 18 Minutes   Serves: 4

Ingredients:

- 1.5 pounds salmon, cut into chunks
- 1/2 cup teriyaki sauce
- 2 tablespoons honey
- 1 tablespoon sesame oil
- 1 teaspoon grated ginger
- Sesame seeds and chopped green onions for garnish

Directions:

1. Heat your Flip Toaster Oven to 400°F in bake mode.
2. In a bowl, mix teriyaki sauce, honey, sesame oil, and grated ginger.
3. Thread salmon chunks onto skewers and place on a baking sheet.
4. Brush the teriyaki mixture over the salmon.
5. Bake for 15 minutes, then switch to broil mode for an additional 3 minutes until the edges caramelize.
6. Garnish with sesame seeds and chopped green onions before serving.

Nutritional Value (Amount per Serving):

Calories: 399; Fat: 19.95; Carb: 15.18; Protein: 38.72

Mediterranean Stuffed Sole

Prep Time: 25 Minutes   Cook Time: 30 Minutes   Serves: 4

Ingredients:

- 4 sole fillets
- 1/2 cup feta cheese, crumbled

- 1/4 cup Kalamata olives, chopped
- 1/4 cup sun-dried tomatoes, chopped
- 2 tablespoons fresh parsley, chopped
- 1 tablespoon olive oil
- Salt and pepper to taste
- Lemon wedges for serving

Directions:

1. Heat your Toaster Oven to 400°F in bake mode.
2. In a bowl, combine feta cheese, Kalamata olives, sun-dried tomatoes, fresh parsley, olive oil, salt, and pepper.
3. Lay sole fillets on a baking sheet and spoon the Mediterranean mixture onto each fillet.
4. Roll up the fillets and secure with toothpicks if needed.
5. Bake for 25-30 minutes until the fish is cooked through and lightly browned.
6. Serve with lemon wedges on the side.

Nutritional Value (Amount per Serving):

Calories: 220; Fat: 11.57; Carb: 5.19; Protein: 23.76

Coconut Shrimp with Mango Salsa

Prep Time: 20 Minutes   Cook Time: 15 Minutes   Serves: 4

Ingredients:

- 1 pound large shrimp, peeled and deveined
- 1 cup shredded coconut
- 1/2 cup panko breadcrumbs
- 2 eggs, beaten
- Salt and pepper to taste
- Mango salsa for serving

Directions:

1. Heat your Toaster Oven to 400°F in bake mode.
2. In separate bowls, place shredded coconut and panko breadcrumbs.
3. Dip each shrimp into beaten eggs, then coat in the coconut mixture.
4. Place the coated shrimp on a baking sheet.
5. Bake for 12-15 minutes until the shrimp are golden and cooked through.
6. Serve with mango salsa on the side.

Nutritional Value (Amount per Serving):

Calories: 119; Fat: 5.3; Carb: 12.43; Protein: 6.15

Blackened Red Snapper Tacos

Prep Time: 15 Minutes   Cook Time: 12 Minutes   Serves: 4

Ingredients:

- 4 red snapper fillets
- 2 tablespoons blackened seasoning
- 1 tablespoon olive oil
- 8 small corn tortillas
- Cabbage slaw (shredded cabbage, lime juice, and cilantro) for serving
- Avocado slices for garnish

Directions:

1. Heat your Toaster Oven to 400°F in broil mode.
2. Rub blackened seasoning over each red snapper fillet.
3. Drizzle olive oil over the fillets.
4. Place the fillets on a broiler pan and broil for 10-12 minutes until the fish is opaque and flakes easily.
5. Warm corn tortillas in the toaster oven for the last 2 minutes.
6. Assemble tacos with red snapper, cabbage slaw, and avocado slices.

Nutritional Value (Amount per Serving):

Calories: 283; Fat: 12.21; Carb: 41.88; Protein: 4.77

Crispy Garlic Parmesan Baked Cod

Prep Time: 15 Minutes   Cook Time: 20 Minutes   Serves: 4

Ingredients:

- 4 cod fillets
- 1/2 cup grated Parmesan cheese
- 1/4 cup breadcrumbs
- 2 tablespoons melted butter
- 2 cloves garlic, minced
- 1 teaspoon dried parsley
- Salt and pepper to taste
- Lemon wedges for serving

Directions:

1. Heat your Toaster Oven to 400°F in bake mode.
2. Mix Parmesan cheese, breadcrumbs, melted butter, minced garlic, dried parsley, salt, and pepper in a bowl.
3. Coat each cod fillet with the mixture and place them on a baking sheet.
4. Bake for 15-20 minutes until the cod is flaky and the topping is golden.
5. Serve with lemon wedges.

Nutritional Value (Amount per Serving):

Calories: 193; Fat: 9.78; Carb: 4.15; Protein: 21.7

Bagel Salmon Avocado Toast

Prep Time: 10 Minutes   Cook Time: 5 Minutes   Serves: 4

Ingredients:

- 4 bagels, halved and toasted
- 8 ounces smoked salmon
- 1 avocado, sliced
- 4 tablespoons cream cheese
- Red onion, thinly sliced
- Capers for garnish
- Fresh dill for garnish
- Lemon wedges for serving

Directions:

1. Heat your Toaster Oven to 350°F in Bagel mode.
2. Toast the bagel halves until golden.
3. Spread cream cheese on each bagel half.
4. Top with smoked salmon, avocado slices, red onion, capers, and fresh dill.
5. Serve with lemon wedges on the side.

Nutritional Value (Amount per Serving):

Calories: 460; Fat: 17.27; Carb: 53.87; Protein: 23.88

Spicy Broiled Shrimp Tostadas

Prep Time: 15 Minutes   Cook Time: 10 Minutes   Serves: 4

Ingredients:

- 1 pound large shrimp, peeled and deveined
- 2 tablespoons olive oil
- 1 teaspoon chili powder
- 1/2 teaspoon cumin
- 1/2 teaspoon smoked paprika
- Salt and pepper to taste
- 8 small tostada shells
- Shredded lettuce, diced tomatoes, and sour cream for topping

Directions:

1. Heat your Toaster Oven to 400°F in broil mode.
2. In a bowl, toss shrimp with olive oil, chili powder, cumin, smoked paprika, salt, and pepper.
3. Arrange shrimp on a broiler pan and broil for 5-7 minutes until shrimp are cooked and slightly charred.
4. Meanwhile, heat tostada shells in the toaster oven.
5. Assemble tostadas with shredded lettuce, diced tomatoes, and a dollop of sour cream.

Nutritional Value (Amount per Serving):

Calories: 352; Fat: 20.44; Carb: 40.97; Protein: 4.75

Lemon Herb Broiled Scallops

Prep Time: 10 Minutes   Cook Time: 8 Minutes   Serves: 4

Ingredients:

- 1 pound sea scallops
- 2 tablespoons olive oil
- 2 tablespoons fresh lemon juice
- 1 teaspoon dried thyme
- 1 teaspoon dried rosemary
- Salt and pepper to taste
- Lemon wedges for serving

Directions:

1. Heat your Toaster Oven to 400°F in broil mode.
2. In a bowl, toss scallops with olive oil, lemon juice, thyme, rosemary, salt, and pepper.
3. Arrange scallops on a broiler pan and broil for 4 minutes per side until they are opaque and lightly browned.
4. Serve with lemon wedges.

Nutritional Value (Amount per Serving):

Calories: 195; Fat: 7.79; Carb: 8.64; Protein: 23.6

Mango Habanero Baked Halibut

Prep Time: 20 Minutes   Cook Time: 20 Minutes   Serves: 4

Ingredients:

- 4 halibut fillets
- 1 cup mango, diced
- 1 habanero pepper, finely chopped
- 2 tablespoons honey
- 2 tablespoons lime juice
- 2 tablespoons chopped cilantro
- Salt and pepper to taste

Directions:

1. Heat your Toaster Oven to 400°F in bake mode.
2. In a bowl, mix mango, habanero pepper, honey, lime juice, cilantro, salt, and pepper.
3. Place halibut fillets on a baking sheet and spoon the mango habanero mixture over each fillet.
4. Bake for 15-20 minutes until the fish is cooked through.
5. Serve with additional mango salsa on top.

Nutritional Value (Amount per Serving):

Calories: 827; Fat: 56.68; Carb: 17.62; Protein: 59.49

Sesame-Crusted Ahi Tuna

Prep Time: 15 Minutes   Cook Time: 12 Minutes   Serves: 4

Ingredients:

- 4 ahi tuna steaks
- 1/4 cup soy sauce
- 2 tablespoons sesame oil
- 2 tablespoons sesame seeds
- 1 tablespoon honey
- 1 tablespoon rice vinegar
- Green onions for garnish

Directions:

1. Heat your Toaster Oven to 400°F in bake mode.
2. In a bowl, mix soy sauce, sesame oil, sesame seeds, honey, and rice vinegar.
3. Coat each tuna steak with the mixture and place them on a baking sheet.
4. Bake for 10-12 minutes for medium-rare, adjusting time for desired doneness.
5. Garnish with sliced green onions before serving.

Nutritional Value (Amount per Serving):

Calories: 669; Fat: 44.92; Carb: 15.04; Protein: 49.01

Cajun Catfish Po' Boys

Prep Time: 15 Minutes   Cook Time: 20 Minutes   Serves: 4

Ingredients:

- 4 catfish fillets
- 2 tablespoons Cajun seasoning
- 1/2 cup mayonnaise
- 1 tablespoon Dijon mustard
- 1 tablespoon lemon juice
- 4 French baguettes, toasted
- Shredded lettuce, sliced tomatoes, and pickles for topping

Directions:

1. Heat your Toaster Oven to 400°F in bake mode.
2. Rub Cajun seasoning evenly over each catfish fillet.
3. In a bowl, mix mayonnaise, Dijon mustard, and lemon juice.
4. Coat each fillet with the mayo mixture and place on a baking sheet.
5. Bake for 15-20 minutes until the catfish is cooked through and the coating

is crispy.
6. Assemble Po' Boy sandwiches with toasted baguettes, shredded lettuce, sliced tomatoes, and pickles.

Nutritional Value (Amount per Serving):

Calories: 508; Fat: 21.11; Carb: 40.6; Protein: 36.76

Mediterranean Stuffed Squid

Prep Time: 25 Minutes   Cook Time: 30 Minutes   Serves: 4

Ingredients:

- 8 small squid tubes
- 1 cup cooked quinoa
- 1/2 cup feta cheese, crumbled
- 1/4 cup Kalamata olives, chopped
- 1/4 cup sun-dried tomatoes, chopped
- 2 tablespoons fresh parsley, chopped
- 1 tablespoon olive oil
- Salt and pepper to taste
- Lemon wedges for serving

Directions:

1. Heat your Toaster Oven to 400°F in bake mode.
2. Rinse squid tubes and pat dry.
3. In a bowl, combine cooked quinoa, feta cheese, Kalamata olives, sun-dried tomatoes, fresh parsley, olive oil, salt, and pepper.
4. Stuff each squid tube with the mixture.
5. Place stuffed squid on a baking sheet and bake for 25-30 minutes until squid is cooked and filling is heated through.
6. Serve with lemon wedges on the side.

Nutritional Value (Amount per Serving):

Calories: 239; Fat: 10.49; Carb: 17.66; Protein: 18.82

Chapter 5: Vegetables and Vegetarian Mains

Baked Mediterranean Vegetables with Quinoa

Prep Time: 15 Minutes   Cook Time: 35 Minutes   Serves: 4-6

Ingredients:

- 2 cups cherry tomatoes, halved
- 1 large zucchini, sliced
- 1 large red bell pepper, cut into strips
- 1 large yellow bell pepper, cut into strips
- 1 red onion, thinly sliced
- 1 cup baby spinach
- 1 cup quinoa, rinsed
- 2 cups vegetable broth
- 3 tablespoons olive oil
- 2 cloves garlic, minced
- 1 teaspoon dried oregano
- Salt and pepper to taste
- Fresh basil leaves for garnish

Directions:

1. Heat your Toaster Oven to 400°F in oven mode.
2. In a medium saucepan, combine quinoa and vegetable broth. Bring to a boil, then reduce heat, cover, and simmer for 15 minutes or until quinoa is cooked. Fluff with a fork and set aside.
3. In a large bowl, toss cherry tomatoes, zucchini, red and yellow bell peppers, and red onion with olive oil, minced garlic, dried oregano, salt, and pepper.
4. Place the prepared vegetables in a baking dish.
5. Flip down the toaster oven for oven mode and bake the vegetables for 20 minutes or until they are tender and slightly browned, stirring halfway through.
6. In a large serving bowl, combine the baked vegetables with cooked quinoa and baby spinach. Toss gently to combine.
7. Garnish with fresh basil leaves.
8. Serve warm as a delicious and nutritious vegetarian main course.

Nutritional Value (Amount per Serving):

Calories: 255; Fat: 10.73; Carb: 34.75; Protein: 7.39

Spinach and Stuffed Portobello Mushrooms

Prep Time: 15 Minutes   Cook Time: 25 Minutes   Serves: 4

Ingredients:

- 4 large portobello mushrooms, stems removed
- 2 tablespoons olive oil

- 1 onion, finely chopped
- 2 cloves garlic, minced
- 2 cups baby spinach, chopped
- 1 cup cremini mushrooms, finely chopped
- 1/2 cup breadcrumbs
- 1/2 cup vegan Parmesan cheese
- Salt and pepper to taste
- Fresh parsley for garnish

Directions:

1. Heat your Toaster Oven to 400°F in oven mode.
2. In a skillet, heat olive oil over medium heat. Saute onions and garlic until softened.
3. Add chopped baby spinach and cremini mushrooms, cooking until the spinach wilts and mushrooms are tender.
4. Stir in breadcrumbs and vegan Parmesan cheese. Season with salt and pepper.
5. Spoon the spinach and mushroom mixture into the portobello mushroom caps.
6. Place stuffed mushrooms on a baking sheet.
7. Flip down the toaster oven for oven mode and bake for 20 minutes or until mushrooms are cooked through.
8. Garnish with fresh parsley.

Nutritional Value (Amount per Serving):

Calories: 161; Fat: 8.22; Carb: 15.16; Protein: 10.27

Pesto Baked Veggie Wrap

Prep Time: 15 Minutes   Cook Time: 20 Minutes   Serves: 4

Ingredients:

- 1 large eggplant, thinly sliced
- 1 large zucchini, thinly sliced
- 1 red bell pepper, sliced
- 1 yellow bell pepper, sliced
- 4 whole-grain wraps
- 1/2 cup vegan pesto
- 1 cup baby spinach
- 1 cup cherry tomatoes, halved
- Salt and pepper to taste

Directions:

1. Heat your Toaster Oven to 400°F in oven mode.
2. Toss eggplant, zucchini, and bell peppers with olive oil, salt, and pepper.
3. Flip down the toaster oven for oven mode and bake the vegetables for 15 minutes or until they are tender and slightly golden.
4. Spread each wrap with a generous layer of vegan pesto.

5. Layer roasted vegetables, baby spinach, and cherry tomatoes on each wrap.
6. Roll up the wraps tightly.
7. Serve immediately for a quick and satisfying vegetarian meal.

Nutritional Value (Amount per Serving):

Calories: 501; Fat: 22.91; Carb: 64.1; Protein: 16.95

Stuffed Bell Peppers with Lentils and Brown Rice

Prep Time: 20 Minutes   Cook Time: 40 Minutes   Serves: 4-6

Ingredients:

- 6 large bell peppers, halved and seeds removed
- 1 cup brown lentils, cooked
- 1 cup cooked brown rice
- 1 cup diced tomatoes
- 1 cup black beans, drained and rinsed
- 1 cup corn kernels
- 1 cup shredded vegan cheese
- 1 teaspoon cumin
- 1 teaspoon chili powder
- Salt and pepper to taste
- Fresh cilantro for garnish

Directions:

1. Heat your Toaster Oven to 390°F in oven mode.
2. In a large bowl, combine cooked lentils, brown rice, diced tomatoes, black beans, corn, vegan cheese, cumin, chili powder, salt, and pepper.
3. Fill each bell pepper half with the lentil and rice mixture.
4. Place the stuffed bell peppers on a baking sheet.
5. Flip down the toaster oven for oven mode and bake for 20 minutes or until the peppers are tender.
6. Garnish with fresh cilantro.
7. Serve warm as a hearty and flavorful vegetarian main dish.

Nutritional Value (Amount per Serving):

Calories: 303; Fat: 7.71; Carb: 48.13; Protein: 13.72

Sweet Potato and Black Bean Quesadillas

Prep Time: 20 Minutes   Cook Time: 25 Minutes   Serves: 4

Ingredients:

- 2 large sweet potatoes, peeled and diced

- 1 can (15 oz) black beans, drained and rinsed
- 1 red bell pepper, diced
- 1 small red onion, finely chopped
- 2 cloves garlic, minced
- 1 teaspoon ground cumin
- 1 teaspoon chili powder
- Salt and pepper to taste
- 4 large whole wheat tortillas
- 2 cups shredded Mexican cheese blend
- Olive oil for brushing
- Salsa and guacamole for serving

Directions:

1. Heat your Toaster Oven to 395°F in oven mode.
2. Toss diced sweet potatoes with olive oil, salt, and pepper.
3. Flip down the toaster oven for oven mode and roast the sweet potatoes for 15 minutes or until they are tender.
4. In a skillet, sauté red bell pepper, red onion, and garlic until softened.
5. Add black beans, roasted sweet potatoes, cumin, chili powder, salt, and pepper. Cook for an additional 5 minutes.
6. Lay out the tortillas and distribute the filling evenly on one half of each tortilla.
7. Sprinkle shredded cheese over the filling and fold the tortillas in half.
8. Place the quesadillas on a baking sheet.
9. Flip down the toaster oven for oven mode and bake for 8-10 minutes or until the cheese is melted and the tortillas are crispy.
10. Cut quesadillas into wedges and serve with salsa and guacamole on the side.

Nutritional Value (Amount per Serving):

Calories: 635; Fat: 28.08; Carb: 68.76; Protein: 29.42

Caprese Stuffed Portobello Mushrooms

Prep Time: 15 Minutes   Cook Time: 20 Minutes   Serves: 4

Ingredients:

- 4 large portobello mushrooms, stems removed
- 1 cup cherry tomatoes, halved
- 1 cup fresh mozzarella balls, halved
- 1/2 cup fresh basil leaves, chopped
- 2 tablespoons balsamic glaze
- 2 tablespoons olive oil
- Salt and pepper to taste

Directions:

1. Heat your Toaster Oven to 400°F in oven mode.
2. Place portobello mushrooms on a baking sheet.
3. Fill each mushroom cap with cherry tomatoes, mozzarella balls, and chopped basil.
4. Drizzle with olive oil and balsamic glaze.
5. Sprinkle with salt and pepper.
6. Bake for 20 minutes or until the mushrooms are tender and the cheese is melted.
7. Garnish with additional fresh basil.
8. Serve warm as a flavorful and elegant vegetarian main.

Nutritional Value (Amount per Serving):

Calories: 107; Fat: 7.32; Carb: 9.64; Protein: 3.09

Veggie Pesto Pasta Bake

Prep Time: 20 Minutes   Cook Time: 20 Minutes   Serves: 6

Ingredients:

- 12 oz penne pasta, cooked al dente
- 2 cups broccoli florets
- 1 cup cherry tomatoes, halved
- 1 bell pepper, diced
- 1 zucchini, sliced
- 1/2 cup sun-dried tomatoes, chopped
- 1 cup shredded mozzarella cheese
- 1/2 cup grated Parmesan cheese
- 1 cup basil pesto
- Salt and pepper to taste

Directions:

1. Heat your Toaster Oven to 400°F in oven mode.
2. Steam broccoli florets until just tender.
3. In a large bowl, combine cooked pasta, steamed broccoli, cherry tomatoes, bell pepper, zucchini, and sun-dried tomatoes.
4. Add basil pesto to the pasta and vegetable mixture. Toss until everything is evenly coated.
5. Transfer the mixture to a baking dish.
6. Sprinkle with shredded mozzarella and grated Parmesan cheese.
7. Bake for 20 minutes or until the cheese is melted and bubbly.
8. Season with salt and pepper to taste.
9. Serve warm as a comforting and flavorful vegetarian pasta bake.

Nutritional Value (Amount per Serving):

Calories: 156; Fat: 3; Carb: 22.33; Protein: 11.38

Cauliflower and Chickpea Curry

Prep Time: 20 Minutes   Cook Time: 25 Minutes   Serves: 4

Ingredients:

- 1 large cauliflower, cut into florets
- 1 can (15 oz) chickpeas, drained and rinsed
- 1 onion, finely chopped
- 3 cloves garlic, minced
- 1 tablespoon fresh ginger, grated
- 1 can (14 oz) diced tomatoes
- 1 can (14 oz) coconut milk
- 2 tablespoons curry powder
- 1 teaspoon ground cumin
- 1 teaspoon ground coriander
- 1/2 teaspoon turmeric
- Salt and pepper to taste
- Fresh cilantro for garnish
- Cooked basmati rice for serving

Directions:

1. Heat your Toaster Oven to 400°F in oven mode.
2. In a large oven-safe skillet, sauté onion, garlic, and ginger until softened.
3. Add cauliflower florets and chickpeas to the skillet, stirring to coat with the aromatic mixture.
4. Stir in diced tomatoes, coconut milk, curry powder, cumin, coriander, turmeric, salt, and pepper.
5. Bake for 25 minutes or until the cauliflower is tender.
6. Garnish with fresh cilantro.
7. Serve over cooked basmati rice as a flavorful and satisfying vegetarian curry.

Nutritional Value (Amount per Serving):

Calories: 415; Fat: 26.68; Carb: 39.94; Protein: 12.6

Zucchini Noodles with Pesto and Cherry Tomatoes

Prep Time: 15 Minutes   Cook Time: 15 Minutes   Serves: 4

Ingredients:

- 4 medium-sized zucchinis, spiralized into noodles
- 1 cup cherry tomatoes, halved
- 1/2 cup pine nuts, toasted

- 1/2 cup grated Parmesan cheese
- 1/2 cup fresh basil pesto
- 2 tablespoons olive oil
- Salt and pepper to taste
- Lemon wedges for serving

Directions:

1. Heat your Toaster Oven to 400°F in oven mode.
2. In a dry skillet, toast pine nuts over medium heat until golden brown. Set aside.
3. Spiralize zucchinis into noodles using a spiralizer. Place zucchini noodles on a baking sheet.
4. Bake for 5-7 minutes or until the noodles are just tender.
5. In a large bowl, toss zucchini noodles with cherry tomatoes, toasted pine nuts, Parmesan cheese, and fresh basil pesto.
6. Drizzle with olive oil. Season with salt and pepper to taste.
7. Serve with lemon wedges for an extra burst of flavor.

Nutritional Value (Amount per Serving):

Calories: 237; Fat: 21.89; Carb: 6.59; Protein: 6.54

Quinoa and Black Bean Stuffed Bell Peppers

Prep Time: 20 Minutes   Cook Time: 30 Minutes   Serves: 4

Ingredients:

- 4 large bell peppers, halved and seeds removed
- 1 cup quinoa, cooked
- 1 can (15 oz) black beans, drained and rinsed
- 1 cup corn kernels
- 1 cup diced tomatoes
- 1/2 cup red onion, finely chopped
- 1 teaspoon ground cumin
- 1 teaspoon chili powder
- Salt and pepper to taste
- 1 cup shredded cheddar cheese
- Fresh cilantro for garnish

Directions:

1. Heat your Toaster Oven to 400°F in oven mode.
2. In a large bowl, combine cooked quinoa, black beans, corn, diced tomatoes, red onion, cumin, chili powder, salt, and pepper.
3. Fill each bell pepper half with the quinoa and black bean mixture.
4. Place the stuffed bell peppers on a baking sheet.

5. Bake for 20 minutes or until the peppers are tender.
6. Sprinkle shredded cheddar cheese on top of each stuffed pepper.
7. Bake for an additional 5-7 minutes or until the cheese is melted and bubbly.
8. Garnish with fresh cilantro.
9. Serve warm as a protein-rich and satisfying vegetarian main.

Nutritional Value (Amount per Serving):

Calories: 430; Fat: 7.33; Carb: 71.78; Protein: 23.12

Ratatouille

Prep Time: 30 Minutes   Cook Time: 45 Minutes   Serves: 6

Ingredients:

- 1 large eggplant, sliced
- 2 medium zucchinis, sliced
- 1 large yellow bell pepper, sliced
- 1 large red bell pepper, sliced
- 1 large red onion, thinly sliced
- 3 cloves garlic, minced
- 1 can (14 oz) crushed tomatoes
- 2 tablespoons tomato paste
- 1 teaspoon dried thyme
- 1 teaspoon dried rosemary
- Salt and pepper to taste
- 3 tablespoons olive oil
- Fresh basil for garnish

Directions:

1. Heat your Toaster Oven to 400°F in oven mode.
2. In a large baking dish, layer sliced eggplant, zucchinis, yellow and red bell peppers, and red onion.
3. In a bowl, mix crushed tomatoes, tomato paste, minced garlic, dried thyme, dried rosemary, salt, and pepper.
4. Pour the tomato mixture over the layered vegetables. Drizzle with olive oil.
5. Bake for 40-45 minutes or until the vegetables are tender.
6. Garnish with fresh basil.
7. Serve as a classic and comforting vegetarian dish.

Nutritional Value (Amount per Serving):

Calories: 114; Fat: 7.12; Carb: 12.61; Protein: 2.31

Spinach and Ricotta Stuffed Shells

Prep Time: 20 Minutes   Cook Time: 25 Minutes   Serves: 4

Ingredients:

- 16 jumbo pasta shells, cooked al dente
- 2 cups ricotta cheese
- 2 cups fresh spinach, chopped

- 1 cup shredded mozzarella cheese
- 1/2 cup grated Parmesan cheese
- 2 cloves garlic, minced
- 1 teaspoon dried oregano
- Salt and pepper to taste
- 2 cups marinara sauce
- Fresh basil for garnish

Directions:

1. Heat your Toaster Oven to 400°F in oven mode.
2. In a bowl, mix ricotta cheese, chopped spinach, mozzarella, Parmesan, minced garlic, dried oregano, salt, and pepper.
3. Fill each cooked pasta shell with the ricotta and spinach mixture.
4. Place the stuffed shells in a baking dish.
5. Bake for 15 minutes or until the cheese is melted and bubbly.
6. Pour marinara sauce over the shells.
7. Garnish with fresh basil.
8. Serve as a comforting and cheesy vegetarian main.

Nutritional Value (Amount per Serving):

Calories: 527; Fat: 22.41; Carb: 50.79; Protein: 32.04

Broccoli and Cheddar Stuffed Potatoes

Prep Time: 15 Minutes   Cook Time: 45 Minutes   Serves: 4

Ingredients:

- 4 large baking potatoes
- 2 cups broccoli florets, steamed
- 1 cup sharp cheddar cheese, shredded
- 1/2 cup sour cream
- 2 tablespoons butter
- Salt and pepper to taste
- Chopped chives for garnish

Directions:

1. Heat your Toaster Oven to 400°F in oven mode.
2. Pierce the potatoes with a fork and place them directly on the oven rack.
3. Bake for 40-45 minutes or until the potatoes are tender.
4. Cut a slit in each baked potato and fluff the insides with a fork.
5. Mix in steamed broccoli, cheddar cheese, sour cream, and butter. Season with salt and pepper.
6. Garnish with chopped chives.
7. Serve as a hearty and cheesy vegetarian main.

Nutritional Value (Amount per Serving):

Calories: 510; Fat: 21.37; Carb: 63.02; Protein: 17.41

Veggie and Quinoa Stuffed Bell Peppers

Prep Time: 20 Minutes   Cook Time: 35 Minutes   Serves: 4

Ingredients:

- 4 large bell peppers, halved and seeds removed
- 1 cup quinoa, cooked
- 1 can (15 oz) black beans, drained and rinsed
- 1 cup corn kernels
- 1 cup cherry tomatoes, diced
- 1/2 cup red onion, finely chopped
- 1 teaspoon ground cumin
- 1 teaspoon chili powder
- Salt and pepper to taste
- 1 cup shredded pepper jack cheese
- Fresh cilantro for garnish

Directions:

1. Heat your Toaster Oven to 400°F in oven mode.
2. In a large bowl, combine cooked quinoa, black beans, corn, diced cherry tomatoes, red onion, cumin, chili powder, salt, and pepper.
3. Fill each bell pepper half with the quinoa and vegetable mixture.
4. Place the stuffed bell peppers on a baking sheet.
5. Bake for 25 minutes or until the peppers are tender.
6. Sprinkle shredded pepper jack cheese on top of each stuffed pepper.
7. Bake for an additional 5-7 minutes or until the cheese is melted and bubbly.
8. Garnish with fresh cilantro.
9. Serve warm as a protein-packed and satisfying vegetarian dish.

Nutritional Value (Amount per Serving):

Calories: 486; Fat: 14.1; Carb: 67.08; Protein: 26.14

Sweet Potato and Black Bean Enchiladas

Prep Time: 25 Minutes   Cook Time: 30 Minutes   Serves: 4

Ingredients:

- 2 large sweet potatoes, peeled and diced
- 1 can (15 oz) black beans, drained and rinsed
- 1 red bell pepper, diced
- 1 small red onion, finely chopped
- 2 cloves garlic, minced

- 1 teaspoon ground cumin
- 1 teaspoon chili powder
- Salt and pepper to taste
- 8 small whole wheat tortillas
- 2 cups enchilada sauce
- 1 cup shredded Mexican cheese blend
- Fresh cilantro for garnish
- Avocado slices for serving

Directions:

1. Heat your Toaster Oven to 400°F in oven mode.
2. Toss diced sweet potatoes with olive oil, cumin, chili powder, salt, and pepper.
3. Roast for 20 minutes or until the sweet potatoes are tender.
4. In a large bowl, mix roasted sweet potatoes, black beans, diced red bell pepper, red onion, and minced garlic.
5. Spoon the filling onto each tortilla and roll them up. Place them seam-side down in a baking dish.
6. Pour enchilada sauce over the rolled tortillas.
7. Sprinkle with shredded Mexican cheese blend.
8. Bake for 10-12 minutes or until the cheese is melted and bubbly.
9. Garnish with fresh cilantro.
10. Serve with avocado slices for a delicious and wholesome vegetarian meal.

Nutritional Value (Amount per Serving):

Calories: 828; Fat: 31.16; Carb: 106.72; Protein: 35.21

Butternut Squash and Sage Risotto

Prep Time: 20 Minutes   Cook Time: 35 Minutes   Serves: 4

Ingredients:

- 1 1/2 cups Arborio rice
- 1/2 cup dry white wine
- 4 cups vegetable broth, heated
- 2 tablespoons olive oil
- 1 small butternut squash, peeled and diced
- 1 onion, finely chopped
- 2 cloves garlic, minced
- 1 teaspoon dried sage
- Salt and pepper to taste
- 1/2 cup grated Parmesan cheese
- Fresh sage leaves for garnish

Directions:

1. Heat your Toaster Oven to 400°F in oven mode.
2. In an oven-safe skillet, heat olive oil. Add chopped onion and garlic, sautéing until softened.
3. Toss diced butternut squash with olive oil, dried sage, salt, and pepper.
4. Roast squashfor 20 minutes or until the squash is tender.
5. Add Arborio rice to the skillet with the sautéed aromatics. Stir to coat the rice.
6. Pour in the white wine and cook until it evaporates.
7. Gradually add heated vegetable broth, one ladle at a time, stirring frequently. Wait until the liquid is absorbed before adding more.
8. Once the rice is almost cooked, fold in the roasted butternut squash and grated Parmesan cheese.
9. Bake the risotto for an additional 10-15 minutes or until it reaches a creamy consistency.
10. Garnish with fresh sage leaves.
11. Serve warm as a rich and comforting vegetarian risotto.

Nutritional Value (Amount per Serving):

Calories: 374; Fat: 23.46; Carb: 43.48; Protein: 14.51

Eggplant Parmesan

Prep Time: 30 Minutes   Cook Time: 45 Minutes   Serves: 4

Ingredients:

- 2 large eggplants, thinly sliced
- Salt for sweating eggplant
- 1 cup all-purpose flour
- 3 large eggs, beaten
- 2 cups breadcrumbs
- 1 cup grated Parmesan cheese
- 2 cups marinara sauce
- 2 cups shredded mozzarella cheese
- Fresh basil for garnish

Directions:

1. Heat your Toaster Oven to 400°F in oven mode.
2. Sprinkle salt over eggplant slices and let them sit for 15 minutes. Pat them dry.
3. Dredge each slice in flour, dip in beaten eggs, then coat with breadcrumbs mixed with grated Parmesan.
4. Place the breaded eggplant slices on a baking sheet.
5. Bake for 20 minutes or until the eggplant is golden and crispy.
6. In a baking dish, layer baked eggplant slices with marinara sauce and shredded mozzarella cheese.
7. Continue to bake for an additional 15-20 minutes or until the cheese is

melted and bubbly.
8. Garnish with fresh basil.
9. Serve warm as a classic and satisfying vegetarian Eggplant Parmesan.

Nutritional Value (Amount per Serving):

Calories: 790; Fat: 43.42; Carb: 48.17; Protein: 52.13

Teriyaki Tofu and Vegetable Skewers

Prep Time: 30 Minutes   Cook Time: 15 Minutes   Serves: 4

Ingredients:

- 1 block firm tofu, pressed and cubed
- 1 bell pepper, cut into chunks
- 1 zucchini, sliced
- 1 red onion, cut into wedges
- 1 cup cherry tomatoes
- 1/2 cup teriyaki sauce
- 2 tablespoons soy sauce
- 1 tablespoon sesame oil
- 1 tablespoon honey
- 1 teaspoon minced ginger
- 1 teaspoon minced garlic
- Wooden skewers, soaked in water

Directions:

1. Heat your Toaster Oven to 400°F in oven mode.
2. In a bowl, mix teriyaki sauce, soy sauce, sesame oil, honey, minced ginger, and minced garlic.
3. Marinate tofu cubes in the sauce for at least 20 minutes.
4. Thread marinated tofu, bell pepper chunks, zucchini slices, red onion wedges, and cherry tomatoes onto soaked wooden skewers.
5. Place skewers on a baking sheet.
6. Bake for 12-15 minutes or until tofu is golden and vegetables are tender.
7. Serve the skewers with rice or noodles for a delicious and protein-packed vegetarian dish.

Nutritional Value (Amount per Serving):

Calories: 191; Fat: 9.2; Carb: 18.37; Protein: 10.99

Caramelized Onion and Gruyere Tart

Prep Time: 30 Minutes   Cook Time: 35 Minutes   Serves: 4

Ingredients:

- 1 sheet puff pastry, thawed
- 2 large onions, thinly sliced
- 2 tablespoons olive oil
- 1 teaspoon sugar
- 1/2 teaspoon balsamic vinegar
- 1 cup Gruyere cheese, grated
- Fresh thyme for garnish
- Salt and pepper to taste

Directions:

1. Heat your Toaster Oven to 400°F in oven mode.
2. In a skillet, heat olive oil over medium heat. Add thinly sliced onions, sugar, and balsamic vinegar.
3. Cook, stirring occasionally, until the onions are golden and caramelized.
4. Roll out the puff pastry on a lightly floured surface to fit your baking sheet.
5. Transfer the rolled-out puff pastry to a baking sheet.
6. Spread the caramelized onions evenly over the puff pastry, leaving a border around the edges.
7. Sprinkle grated Gruyere cheese over the onions.
8. Season with salt and pepper.
9. Bake for 25-30 minutes or until the pastry is golden and the cheese is melted.
10. Garnish with fresh thyme.
11. Serve the Caramelized Onion and Gruyere Tart as a savory and sophisticated vegetarian option.

Nutritional Value (Amount per Serving):

Calories: 531; Fat: 41.33; Carb: 22.84; Protein: 18.18

Chapter 6: Appetizers and Snacks

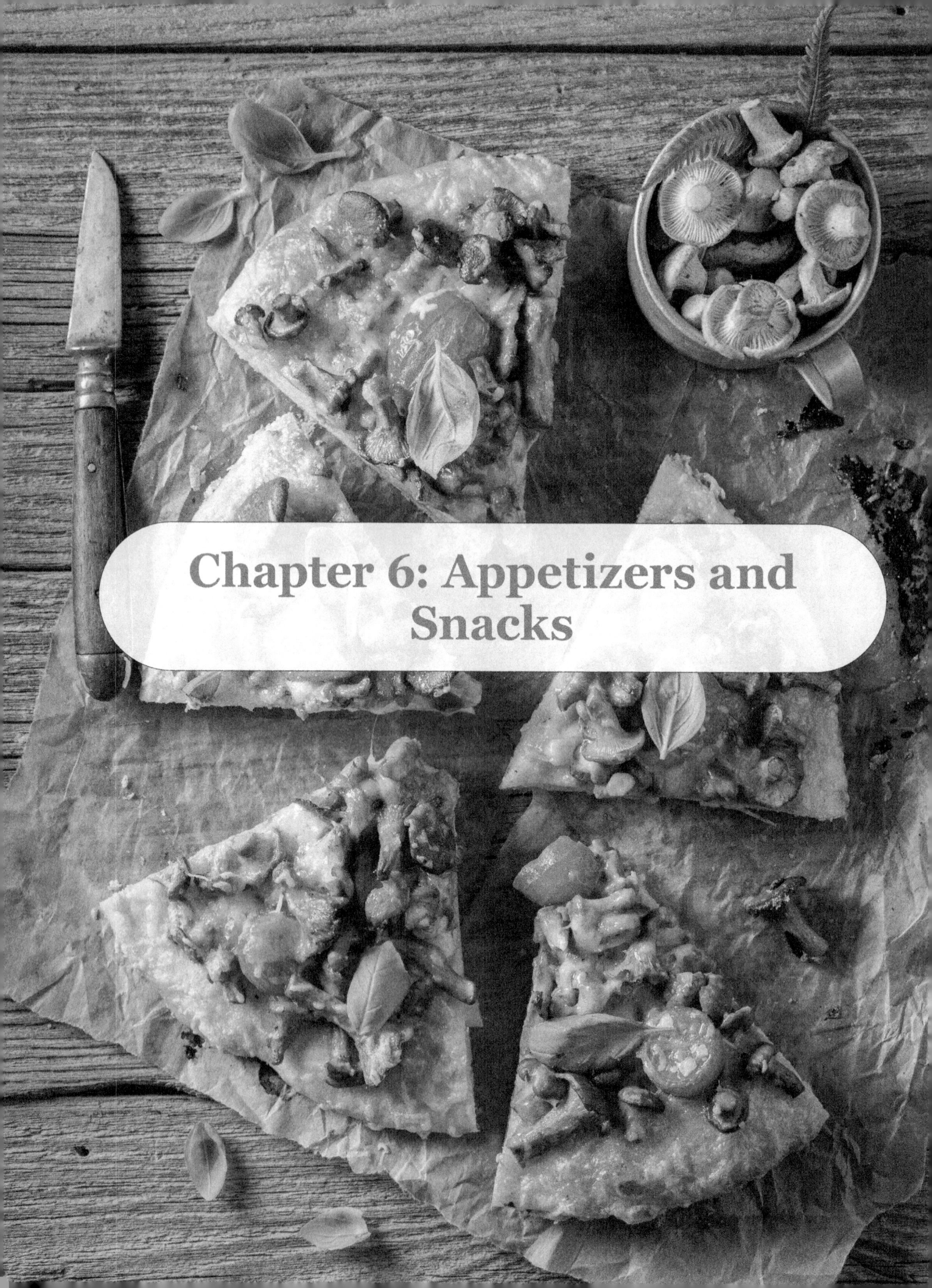

Lentil Loaf

Prep Time: 35 Minutes   Cook Time: 1 Hour 30 Minutes   Serves: 6

Ingredients:

- 3/4 cup brown lentils, rinsed
- 1 can (14-1/2 ounces) vegetable broth
- 1 tablespoon olive oil
- 1-3/4 cups shredded carrots
- 1 cup finely chopped onion
- 1 cup chopped fresh mushrooms
- 2 tablespoons minced fresh basil or 2 teaspoons dried basil
- 1 tablespoon minced fresh parsley
- 1 cup shredded part-skim mozzarella cheese
- 1/2 cup cooked brown rice
- 1 large egg
- 1 large egg white
- 1/2 teaspoon salt
- 1/2 teaspoon garlic powder
- 1/4 teaspoon pepper
- 2 tablespoons tomato paste
- 2 tablespoons water

Directions:

1. Place lentils and broth in a small saucepan; bring to a boil. Reduce heat; simmer, covered, until tender, about 30 minutes.
2. Heat oven to 350°F. Line a loaf pan with parchment, letting ends extend up sides. Coat paper with cooking spray.
3. In a large skillet, heat oil over medium heat; saute carrots, onion and mushrooms until tender, about 10 minutes. Stir in herbs. Transfer to a large bowl; cool slightly.
4. Add cheese, rice, egg, egg white, seasonings and lentils to vegetables; mix well. Transfer to prepared loaf pan. Mix tomato paste and water; spread over loaf.
5. Bake until a thermometer inserted into the center reads 160°F, 45-50 minutes. Let stand 10 minutes before slicing.

Nutritional Value (Amount per Serving):

Calories: 181; Fat: 6.88; Carb: 21.99; Protein: 9

Cheesy Garlic Bread Bites

Prep Time: 15 Minutes   Cook Time: 20 Minutes   Serves: 6-8

Ingredients:

- 1 loaf of French bread
- 1/2 cup unsalted butter, softened
- 4 cloves garlic, minced
- 1 cup shredded mozzarella cheese
- 1/4 cup grated Parmesan cheese
- 1 tablespoon fresh parsley, chopped
- Salt and pepper to taste

Directions:

1. Heat your Toaster Oven to 400°F in oven mode.
2. Cut the French bread into bite-sized cubes.
3. In a bowl, mix the softened butter, minced garlic, chopped parsley, salt, and pepper.
4. Toss the bread cubes in the garlic butter mixture until evenly coated.
5. Place the coated bread cubes on a baking sheet in a single layer.
6. Sprinkle the shredded mozzarella and grated Parmesan cheese evenly over the bread cubes.
7. Flip down to oven mode.
8. Bake at 400°F for about 15 minutes or until the cheese is melted and the bread cubes are golden brown.
9. Remove from the toaster oven and let it cool for a few minutes.
10. Serve warm and enjoy your Cheesy Garlic Bread Bites!

Nutritional Value (Amount per Serving):

Calories: 229; Fat: 11.17; Carb: 22.04; Protein: 10.45

Caprese Skewers

Prep Time: 15 Minutes   Cook Time: 5 Minutes   Serves: 4-6

Ingredients:

- 24 cherry tomatoes
- 24 fresh mozzarella balls
- 24 fresh basil leaves
- Balsamic glaze for drizzling
- Salt and pepper to taste
- Wooden skewers

Directions:

1. Thread a cherry tomato, a mozzarella ball, and a basil leaf onto each skewer.
2. Arrange the skewers on the flip-down oven rack.
3. Sprinkle with salt and pepper, then drizzle with balsamic glaze.
4. Broil in the Flip Toaster Oven for 3-5 minutes or until the cheese begins to melt.
5. Serve immediately.

Nutritional Value (Amount per Serving):

Calories: 101; Fat: 0.66; Carb: 24.34; Protein: 2.64

Mini Margherita Pizzas

Prep Time: 20 Minutes   Cook Time: 15 Minutes   Serves: 4-6

Ingredients:

- 1 package mini pizza dough rounds
- 1 cup marinara sauce
- 1 cup fresh mozzarella, sliced
- 1 cup cherry tomatoes, halved
- Fresh basil leaves for garnish
- Olive oil for drizzling
- Salt and pepper to taste

Directions:

1. Preheat the Flip Toaster Oven to 400°F in bake mode.
2. Place mini pizza dough rounds on the flip-down oven rack.
3. Spread a spoonful of marinara sauce on each round, then top with mozzarella slices and cherry tomato halves.
4. Drizzle with olive oil and sprinkle with salt and pepper.
5. Bake for 12-15 minutes or until the crust is golden and the cheese is melted.
6. Garnish with fresh basil leaves before serving.

Nutritional Value (Amount per Serving):

Calories: 422; Fat: 16.91; Carb: 45.21; Protein: 22.81

Buffalo Cauliflower Bites

Prep Time: 15 Minutes   Cook Time: 25 Minutes   Serves: 4-6

Ingredients:

- 1 head cauliflower, cut into florets
- 1 cup buffalo sauce
- 1/2 cup flour
- 1/2 cup water
- 1 teaspoon garlic powder
- 1/2 teaspoon onion powder
- Ranch or blue cheese dressing for dipping

Directions:

1. Heat the Flip Toaster Oven to 400°F in bake mode.
2. In a bowl, whisk together the flour, water, garlic powder, and onion powder to create a batter.
3. Dip each cauliflower floret into the batter, ensuring it's well-coated, and place on the flip-down oven rack.
4. Bake for 20-25 minutes or until the cauliflower is golden and crispy.
5. Toss the baked cauliflower in buffalo sauce and serve with ranch or blue cheese dressing.

Nutritional Value (Amount per Serving):

Calories: 215; Fat: 6.43; Carb: 36.68; Protein: 3.06

Avocado and Black Bean Quesadillas

Prep Time: 15 Minutes   Cook Time: 10 Minutes   Serves: 4-6

Ingredients:

- 4 large flour tortillas
- 2 ripe avocados, mashed
- 1 cup black beans, drained and rinsed
- 1 cup shredded Monterey Jack cheese
- 1/2 cup diced red onion
- 1/4 cup chopped cilantro
- 1 lime, juiced
- Salt and pepper to taste
- Sour cream and salsa for serving

Directions:

1. Heat the Toaster Oven to 375°F in bake mode.
2. Lay out the tortillas and spread mashed avocado evenly over one half of each tortilla.
3. Add black beans, Monterey Jack cheese, red onion, and cilantro on top of the avocado.
4. Squeeze lime juice over the filling and season with salt and pepper.
5. Fold the tortillas in half and place them on the flip-down oven rack.
6. Bake for 8-10 minutes or until the tortillas are crisp and the cheese is melted.
7. Serve with sour cream and salsa.

Nutritional Value (Amount per Serving):

Calories: 414; Fat: 23.81; Carb: 37.93; Protein: 15.25

Mini Meatball Sliders

Prep Time: 20 Minutes   Cook Time: 20 Minutes   Serves: 4-6

Ingredients:

- 24 small meatballs (homemade or store-bought)
- 12 slider buns, split
- 1 cup marinara sauce
- 1 cup shredded mozzarella cheese
- Fresh basil leaves for garnish

Directions:

1. Heat the Toaster Oven to 375°F in bake mode.
2. Heat the meatballs according to package instructions or make your own.
3. Place the bottom halves of the slider buns on the flip-down oven rack.
4. Top each bun with a meatball, spoon marinara sauce over each, and sprinkle with mozzarella cheese.
5. Place the top halves of the buns over the meatballs.
6. Bake for 15-20 minutes or until the cheese is melted and bubbly.
7. Garnish with fresh basil leaves before serving.

Nutritional Value (Amount per Serving):

Calories: 374; Fat: 13.63; Carb: 23.87; Protein: 39.09

Red Pepper Hummus

Prep Time: 10 Minutes   Cook Time: 15 Minutes   Serves: 6-8

Ingredients:

- 2 cans (15 oz each) chickpeas, drained and rinsed
- 1 cup roasted red peppers, drained
- 1/3 cup tahini
- 2 cloves garlic, minced
- 1/4 cup olive oil
- Juice of 1 lemon
- Salt and cayenne pepper to taste
- Pita bread or vegetable sticks for serving

Directions:

1. Heat the Toaster Oven to 375°F in bake mode.
2. In a food processor, combine chickpeas, roasted red peppers, tahini, garlic, olive oil, and lemon juice.
3. Blend until smooth, adding more olive oil if needed.
4. Season with salt and a pinch of cayenne pepper to taste.
5. Transfer the hummus to an oven-safe dish and bake for 10-15 minutes.
6. Serve warm with pita bread or vegetable sticks.

Nutritional Value (Amount per Serving):

Calories: 273; Fat: 16.93; Carb: 23.98; Protein: 8.86

Bacon-Wrapped Jalapeño Poppers

Prep Time: 20 Minutes   Cook Time: 20 Minutes   Serves: 4-6

Ingredients:

- 12 large jalapeño peppers, halved and seeds removed
- 8 oz cream cheese, softened
- 1 cup shredded cheddar cheese
- 12 slices bacon, cut in half
- Toothpicks

Directions:

1. Heat the Toaster Oven to 375°F in bake mode.
2. In a bowl, mix cream cheese and shredded cheddar until well combined.
3. Spoon the cheese mixture into each jalapeño half.
4. Wrap each jalapeño half with a half-slice of bacon and secure with toothpicks.
5. Place the bacon-wrapped jalapeños on the flip-down oven rack.
6. Bake for 15-20 minutes or until the bacon is crispy.
7. Allow to cool slightly before serving.

Nutritional Value (Amount per Serving):

Calories: 491; Fat: 40.71; Carb: 15.97; Protein: 17.76

Baked Zucchini Fries

Prep Time: 15 Minutes   Cook Time: 20 Minutes   Serves: 4-6

Ingredients:

- 2 large zucchini, cut into fries
- 1 cup breadcrumbs
- 1/2 cup grated Parmesan cheese
- 2 eggs, beaten
- 1 teaspoon garlic powder
- 1/2 teaspoon dried oregano
- Marinara sauce for dipping

Directions:

1. Heat the Toaster Oven to 400°F in bake mode.
2. In one bowl, mix breadcrumbs, Parmesan cheese, garlic powder, and dried oregano.
3. Dip zucchini fries into beaten eggs, then coat with the breadcrumb mixture.
4. Place the coated zucchini fries on the flip-down oven rack.
5. Bake for 15-20 minutes or until golden and crispy.
6. Serve with marinara sauce for dipping.

Nutritional Value (Amount per Serving):

Calories: 120; Fat: 7.07; Carb: 6.72; Protein: 8.19

Teriyaki Chicken Skewers

Prep Time: 20 Minutes   Cook Time: 15 Minutes   Serves: 4-6

Ingredients:

- 2 boneless, skinless chicken breasts, cut into chunks
- 1/2 cup teriyaki sauce
- 1/4 cup soy sauce
- 2 tablespoons honey
- 1 tablespoon sesame oil
- 2 cloves garlic, minced
- 1 teaspoon grated ginger
- Wooden skewers

Directions:

1. Heat the Toaster Oven to 400°F in bake mode.
2. In a bowl, mix together teriyaki sauce, soy sauce, honey, sesame oil, garlic, and ginger.
3. Thread chicken chunks onto wooden skewers and place them on the flip-down oven rack.
4. Brush the chicken skewers with the teriyaki mixture.
5. Bake for 12-15 minutes or until the chicken is cooked through.
6. Serve hot, garnished with sesame seeds and chopped green onions.

Nutritional Value (Amount per Serving):

Calories: 272; Fat: 10.2; Carb: 34; Protein: 11.14

Mediterranean Stuffed Mini Peppers

Prep Time: 15 Minutes   Cook Time: 20 Minutes   Serves: 4-6

Ingredients:

- 12 mini bell peppers, halved and seeds removed
- 1 cup hummus
- 1/2 cup cherry tomatoes, halved
- 1/4 cup Kalamata olives, chopped
- 1/4 cup crumbled feta cheese
- Fresh parsley for garnish

Directions:

1. Heat the Toaster Oven to 375°F in bake mode.
2. Fill each mini pepper half with hummus.
3. Top with cherry tomatoes, Kalamata olives, and crumbled feta cheese.
4. Place the stuffed peppers on the flip-down oven rack.

5. Bake for 15-20 minutes or until the peppers are tender.
6. Garnish with fresh parsley before serving.

Nutritional Value (Amount per Serving):

Calories: 158; Fat: 6.76; Carb: 20.99; Protein: 5.69

Stuffed Jalapeño Popper Dip

Prep Time: 15 Minutes   Cook Time: 20 Minutes   Serves: 6-8

Ingredients:

- 8 oz cream cheese, softened
- 1 cup shredded cheddar cheese
- 1/2 cup mayonnaise
- 1/2 cup sour cream
- 6 slices bacon, cooked and crumbled
- 6 jalapeños, seeded and diced
- 1 cup breadcrumbs
- Tortilla chips for dipping

Directions:

1. Heat the Toaster Oven to 375°F in bake mode.
2. In a bowl, mix cream cheese, cheddar cheese, mayonnaise, sour cream, bacon, and diced jalapeños.
3. Transfer the mixture to an oven-safe dish and top with breadcrumbs.
4. Bake for 15-20 minutes or until the dip is hot and bubbly.
5. Serve with tortilla chips.

Nutritional Value (Amount per Serving):

Calories: 364; Fat: 32.1; Carb: 8.29; Protein: 11.82

Cucumber Bites with Dill Cream Cheese

Prep Time: 15 Minutes   Cook Time: 5 Minutes   Serves: 4-6

Ingredients:

- 2 large cucumbers, sliced into rounds
- 8 oz cream cheese, softened
- 2 tablespoons fresh dill, chopped
- 1 tablespoon lemon juice
- Salt and pepper to taste
- Smoked salmon or cherry tomatoes for topping

Directions:

1. Heat the Toaster Oven to 375°F in bake mode.
2. In a bowl, mix cream cheese, fresh dill, lemon juice, salt, and pepper.
3. Spread a dollop of the cream cheese mixture onto each cucumber round.
4. Top with smoked salmon or a halved cherry tomato.

5. Place the cucumber bites on the flip-down oven rack.
6. Bake for 3-5 minutes or until the cream cheese is slightly warmed.
7. Serve immediately.

Nutritional Value (Amount per Serving):

Calories: 148; Fat: 13.39; Carb: 4.43; Protein: 3.87

Pizza Stuffed Mushrooms

Prep Time: 20 Minutes   Cook Time: 15 Minutes   Serves: 4-6

Ingredients:

- 24 large mushrooms, cleaned and stems removed
- 1 cup pizza sauce
- 1 cup shredded mozzarella cheese
- 1/2 cup pepperoni slices, chopped
- 1/4 cup grated Parmesan cheese
- 1 teaspoon dried oregano
- Fresh basil for garnish

Directions:

1. Heat the Toaster Oven to 375°F in bake mode.
2. Fill each mushroom cap with pizza sauce, mozzarella cheese, chopped pepperoni, and grated Parmesan.
3. Sprinkle dried oregano over the stuffed mushrooms.
4. Place the mushrooms on the flip-down oven rack.
5. Bake for 12-15 minutes or until the cheese is melted and bubbly.
6. Garnish with fresh basil before serving.

Nutritional Value (Amount per Serving):

Calories: 106; Fat: 2.44; Carb: 9.59; Protein: 13.16

Greek Salad Skewers

Prep Time: 15 Minutes   Cook Time: 5 Minutes   Serves: 4-6

Ingredients:

- 24 cherry tomatoes
- 1 cucumber, cut into chunks
- 1 cup feta cheese, cubed
- 1/2 cup Kalamata olives
- 1/4 cup red onion, thinly sliced
- Greek salad dressing for drizzling
- Wooden skewers

Directions:

1. Thread a cherry tomato, a cucumber chunk, a cube of feta, an olive, and a

slice of red onion onto each skewer.
2. Arrange the skewers on the flip-down oven rack.
3. Drizzle with Greek salad dressing. Heat the Toaster Oven to 350°F.
4. Broil for 3-5 minutes or until the cheese begins to soften.
5. Serve immediately.

Nutritional Value (Amount per Serving):

Calories: 313; Fat: 26.97; Carb: 13.26; Protein: 6.01

BBQ Chicken Flatbread

Prep Time: 15 Minutes   Cook Time: 15 Minutes   Serves: 4-6

Ingredients:

- 2 flatbreads
- 1 cup cooked chicken, shredded
- 1/2 cup barbecue sauce
- 1 cup shredded mozzarella cheese
- 1/4 cup red onion, thinly sliced
- 1/4 cup fresh cilantro, chopped

Directions:

1. Heat the Toaster Oven to 375°F in bake mode.
2. Place flatbreads on the flip-down oven rack.
3. In a bowl, mix shredded chicken with barbecue sauce.
4. Spread the barbecue chicken evenly over the flatbreads.
5. Sprinkle with mozzarella cheese and red onion slices.
6. Bake for 12-15 minutes or until the cheese is melted and bubbly.
7. Garnish with fresh cilantro before serving.

Nutritional Value (Amount per Serving):

Calories: 411; Fat: 16.46; Carb: 45.51; Protein: 20

Mini Shrimp Tacos

Prep Time: 20 Minutes   Cook Time: 15 Minutes   Serves: 4-6

Ingredients:

- 1 pound small shrimp, peeled and deveined
- 2 tablespoons taco seasoning
- 1 tablespoon olive oil
- Mini flour tortillas
- 1 cup shredded lettuce

- 1 cup diced tomatoes
- 1/2 cup shredded cheddar cheese
- 1/4 cup sour cream
- Fresh cilantro for garnish

Directions:

1. Heat the Toaster Oven to 375°F in bake mode.
2. In a bowl, toss shrimp with taco seasoning and olive oil.
3. Place the seasoned shrimp on the flip-down oven rack.
4. Bake for 10-12 minutes or until the shrimp are cooked through.
5. Assemble mini tacos with shrimp, lettuce, tomatoes, cheese, sour cream, and garnish with fresh cilantro.

Nutritional Value (Amount per Serving):

Calories: 190; Fat: 7.51; Carb: 12.48; Protein: 17.22

Greek Spanakopita Triangles

Prep Time: 30 Minutes   Cook Time: 20 Minutes   Serves: 4-6

Ingredients:

- 1 package phyllo dough, thawed
- 2 cups fresh spinach, chopped
- 1 cup feta cheese, crumbled
- 1/2 cup ricotta cheese
- 1/4 cup fresh dill, chopped
- 1/4 cup green onions, chopped
- 1/4 cup melted butter

Directions:

1. Heat the Toaster Oven to 375°F in bake mode.
2. In a bowl, combine chopped spinach, feta cheese, ricotta cheese, dill, and green onions.
3. Lay out a sheet of phyllo dough and brush with melted butter.
4. Place a small spoonful of the spinach mixture at one end of the phyllo sheet.
5. Fold the phyllo dough over the filling to form a triangle.
6. Continue folding in a triangle shape until you reach the end of the sheet.
7. Place the triangles on the flip-down oven rack.
8. Bake for 15-20 minutes or until the triangles are golden and crispy.
9. Allow to cool slightly before serving.

Nutritional Value (Amount per Serving):

Calories: 219; Fat: 19.11; Carb: 4.66; Protein: 7.81

Southwest Quinoa Stuffed Peppers

Prep Time: 15 Minutes   Cook Time: 25 Minutes   Serves: 4-6

Ingredients:

- 6 bell peppers, halved and seeds removed
- 1 cup cooked quinoa
- 1 cup black beans, drained and rinsed
- 1 cup corn kernels
- 1 cup diced tomatoes
- 1/2 cup shredded cheddar cheese
- 1 teaspoon ground cumin
- 1/2 teaspoon chili powder
- Fresh cilantro for garnish
- Lime wedges for serving

Directions:

1. Heat the Toaster Oven to 375°F in bake mode.
2. Place bell pepper halves on the flip-down oven rack.
3. In a bowl, mix quinoa, black beans, corn, diced tomatoes, cheddar cheese, cumin, and chili powder.
4. Spoon the quinoa mixture into each bell pepper half.
5. Bake for 20-25 minutes or until the peppers are tender.
6. Garnish with fresh cilantro and serve with lime wedges.

Nutritional Value (Amount per Serving):

Calories: 186; Fat: 3.7; Carb: 30.95; Protein: 10.09

Bruschetta with Balsamic Glaze

Prep Time: 15 Minutes   Cook Time: 10 Minutes   Serves: 4-6

Ingredients:

- 1 French baguette, sliced
- 4 large tomatoes, diced
- 1/2 cup fresh basil, chopped
- 3 cloves garlic, minced
- 1/4 cup extra virgin olive oil
- Salt and pepper to taste
- Balsamic glaze for drizzling

Directions:

1. Heat the Toaster Oven to 375°F in bake mode.
2. Arrange baguette slices on the flip-down oven rack.
3. In a bowl, combine diced tomatoes, basil, garlic, olive oil, salt, and pepper.
4. Spoon the tomato mixture onto each baguette slice.
5. Drizzle with balsamic glaze.
6. Bake for 8-10 minutes or until the edges of the baguette are golden.
7. Serve warm.

Nutritional Value (Amount per Serving):

Calories: 176; Fat: 7.78; Carb: 22.65; Protein: 5.3

Mediterranean Pita Nachos

Prep Time: 15 Minutes   Cook Time: 10 Minutes   Serves: 4-6

Ingredients:

- 4 whole wheat pitas, cut into triangles
- 1 cup hummus
- 1 cup cherry tomatoes, halved
- 1/2 cup cucumber, diced
- 1/4 cup Kalamata olives, sliced
- 1/4 cup red onion, finely chopped
- 1/2 cup crumbled feta cheese
- Fresh parsley for garnish
- Olive oil for drizzling

Directions:

1. Heat the Toaster Oven to 375°F in bake mode.
2. Arrange pita triangles on the flip-down oven rack.
3. Drizzle the pita triangles with olive oil and bake for 5-7 minutes or until they are crispy.
4. Once the pitas are crispy, spread hummus over each triangle.
5. Top with cherry tomatoes, cucumber, Kalamata olives, red onion, and crumbled feta.
6. Return to the oven for 3-5 minutes to warm the toppings.
7. Garnish with fresh parsley before serving.

Nutritional Value (Amount per Serving):

Calories: 252; Fat: 14.48; Carb: 24.82; Protein: 7.11

Chapter 7: Desserts and Baked Goods

Chocolate Chip Cookies

Prep Time: 15 Minutes   Cook Time: 20 Minutes   Serves: 12

Ingredients:

- 1 cup unsalted butter, softened
- 1 cup granulated sugar
- 1 cup brown sugar, packed
- 2 large eggs
- 1 teaspoon vanilla extract
- 3 cups all-purpose flour
- 1 teaspoon baking soda
- 1/2 teaspoon baking powder
- 1/2 teaspoon salt
- 2 cups chocolate chips

Directions:

1. Flip down the toaster oven to the "Bake" mode, and set the temperature to 350°F.
2. In a large mixing bowl, cream together the softened butter, granulated sugar, and brown sugar until light and fluffy.
3. Add the eggs one at a time, beating well after each addition. Stir in the vanilla extract.
4. In a separate bowl, whisk together the flour, baking soda, baking powder, and salt. Gradually add the dry ingredients to the wet ingredients, mixing until just combined.
5. Fold in the chocolate chips until evenly distributed in the dough.
6. Scoop tablespoon-sized portions of dough and roll them into balls. Place them on a parchment-lined baking sheet, leaving enough space between each.
7. Place the baking sheet in the preheated toaster oven.
8. Bake for 10-12 minutes or until the edges are golden brown.
9. Remove the cookies from the toaster oven and let them cool on the baking sheet for 5 minutes.
10. Transfer the cookies to a wire rack to cool completely before serving.

Nutritional Value (Amount per Serving):

Calories: 437; Fat: 16.8; Carb: 66.45; Protein: 5.54

Berry Crumble

Prep Time: 15 Minutes   Cook Time: 30 Minutes   Serves: 6

Ingredients:

- 4 cups mixed berries (strawberries, blueberries, raspberries)
- 1/2 cup granulated sugar
- 1 tablespoon lemon juice
- 1 cup old-fashioned oats
- 1/2 cup all-purpose flour
- 1/2 cup brown sugar, packed
- 1/4 cup unsalted butter, melted

- 1/2 teaspoon cinnamon
- Pinch of salt

Directions:

1. Flip down the toaster oven to the "Bake" mode, and set the temperature to 375°F.
2. In a bowl, combine the mixed berries, granulated sugar, and lemon juice. Toss until the berries are coated.
3. In another bowl, mix oats, flour, brown sugar, melted butter, cinnamon, and a pinch of salt until crumbly.
4. Spread the berry mixture in a baking dish.
5. Sprinkle the crumble topping evenly over the berries.
6. Bake for 25-30 minutes or until the topping is golden brown, and the berries are bubbly.
7. Allow the berry crumble to cool slightly before serving. It pairs well with a scoop of vanilla ice cream.

Nutritional Value (Amount per Serving):

Calories: 499; Fat: 19.38; Carb: 82.51; Protein: 6.56

Banana Nut Muffins

Prep Time: 15 Minutes   Cook Time: 25 Minutes   Serves: 8

Ingredients:

- 2 ripe bananas, mashed
- 1/2 cup unsalted butter, melted
- 1/2 cup granulated sugar
- 1 large egg
- 1 teaspoon vanilla extract
- 1 1/2 cups all-purpose flour
- 1 teaspoon baking powder
- 1/2 teaspoon baking soda
- 1/4 teaspoon salt
- 1/2 cup chopped nuts (walnuts or pecans)

Directions:

1. Flip down the toaster oven to the "Bake" mode, and heat to 350°F.
2. In a bowl, combine mashed bananas, melted butter, granulated sugar, egg, and vanilla extract.
3. In a separate bowl, whisk together the flour, baking powder, baking soda, and salt.
4. Gradually add the dry ingredients to the wet ingredients, stirring until just combined.
5. Fold in the chopped nuts. Spoon the batter into muffin cups, filling each about 2/3 full.
6. Bake for 20-25 minutes or until a toothpick inserted into the center comes out clean.
7. Allow the muffins to cool in the pan for 5 minutes, then transfer to a wire

rack to cool completely.

Nutritional Value (Amount per Serving):

Calories: 282; Fat: 16.31; Carb: 31.17; Protein: 4.14

Lemon Blueberry Pound Cake

Prep Time: 20 Minutes   Cook Time: 45 Minutes   Serves: 8-10

Ingredients:

- 1 cup unsalted butter, softened
- 2 cups granulated sugar
- 4 large eggs
- 1 teaspoon vanilla extract
- 3 cups all-purpose flour
- 1 tablespoon baking powder
- 1/2 teaspoon salt
- 1 cup sour cream
- Zest of 2 lemons
- 2 cups fresh blueberries

Directions:

1. Flip down the toaster oven to the "Bake" mode, and heat to 350°F.
2. In a large bowl, cream together the softened butter and sugar until light and fluffy.
3. Add the eggs one at a time, beating well after each addition. Stir in the vanilla extract.
4. In a separate bowl, whisk together the flour, baking powder, and salt.
5. Gradually add the dry ingredients to the wet ingredients, alternating with the sour cream. Begin and end with the dry ingredients.
6. Fold in the lemon zest and blueberries. Transfer the batter to a greased and floured loaf pan.
7. Bake for 40-45 minutes or until a toothpick inserted into the center comes out clean.
8. Allow the pound cake to cool in the pan for 10 minutes before transferring to a wire rack to cool completely.
9. Optionally, drizzle with a simple lemon glaze made with powdered sugar and lemon juice.

Nutritional Value (Amount per Serving):

Calories: 477; Fat: 19.06; Carb: 70.18; Protein: 7.63

Apple Cinnamon Baked Oatmeal

Prep Time: 15 Minutes   Cook Time: 40 Minutes   Serves: 6

Ingredients:

- 2 cups old-fashioned oats

- 1/2 cup chopped nuts (pecans or almonds)
- 2 cups milk
- 1/4 cup maple syrup
- 2 tablespoons melted butter
- 1 large egg
- 1 teaspoon vanilla extract
- 1 teaspoon ground cinnamon
- 1/2 teaspoon baking powder
- 1/4 teaspoon salt
- 2 medium apples, peeled and diced

Directions:

1. Flip down the toaster oven to the "Bake" mode, and heat to 375°F.
2. In a bowl, mix together oats, chopped nuts, cinnamon, baking powder, and salt.
3. In another bowl, whisk together milk, maple syrup, melted butter, egg, and vanilla extract.
4. Add the wet ingredients to the dry ingredients and mix until well combined.
5. Fold in the diced apples. Pour the mixture into a greased baking dish.
6. Bake for 35-40 minutes or until the top is golden brown, and the oatmeal is set.
7. Allow the baked oatmeal to cool for a few minutes before slicing and serving.

Nutritional Value (Amount per Serving):

Calories: 319; Fat: 18.03; Carb: 44.1; Protein: 9.54

Mini Cheesecakes

Prep Time: 20 Minutes   Cook Time: 25 Minutes   Serves: 6

Ingredients:

- 1 cup graham cracker crumbs
- 3 tablespoons unsalted butter, melted
- 16 ounces cream cheese, softened
- 1/2 cup granulated sugar
- 2 large eggs
- 1 teaspoon vanilla extract
- 1/4 cup sour cream
- Fruit preserves or fresh berries for topping

Directions:

1. Flip down the toaster oven to the "Bake" mode.
2. Set the temperature to 325°F.

3. In a bowl, mix graham cracker crumbs with melted butter. Press the mixture into the bottom of each mini cheesecake cup.
4. In a large bowl, beat the cream cheese until smooth. Add sugar, eggs, vanilla extract, and sour cream. Mix until well combined.
5. Spoon the cream cheese mixture over the crust in each cup.
6. Bake for 20-25 minutes or until the edges are set but the centers are slightly jiggly.
7. Allow the mini cheesecakes to cool in the pan for 10 minutes, then transfer to a wire rack.
8. Once cooled, top each cheesecake with fruit preserves or fresh berries.

Nutritional Value (Amount per Serving):

Calories: 345; Fat: 28.88; Carb: 14.99; Protein: 7.14

Cinnamon Sugar Donuts

Prep Time: 15 Minutes   Cook Time: 15 Minutes   Serves: 6

Ingredients:
- 1 cup all-purpose flour
- 1/2 cup granulated sugar
- 1 teaspoon baking powder
- 1/2 teaspoon ground cinnamon
- 1/2 cup milk
- 1 large egg
- 2 tablespoons unsalted butter, melted
- 1 teaspoon vanilla extract
- For Coating: 1/4 cup unsalted butter (melted), 1/2 cup granulated sugar, 1 teaspoon ground cinnamon

Directions:
1. Flip down the toaster oven to the "Bake" mode.
2. Set the temperature to 375°F.
3. In a bowl, whisk together flour, sugar, baking powder, and cinnamon.
4. In another bowl, whisk together milk, egg, melted butter, and vanilla extract.
5. Combine wet and dry ingredients until just mixed.
6. Spoon the batter into a greased donut pan.
7. Bake for 10-12 minutes or until a toothpick inserted comes out clean.
8. While the donuts are still warm, dip each in melted butter and then coat in a mixture of sugar and cinnamon.

Nutritional Value (Amount per Serving):

Calories: 203; Fat: 9.34; Carb: 25.94; Protein: 3.71

Peach Cobbler

Prep Time: 20 Minutes   Cook Time: 30 Minutes   Serves: 8

Ingredients:

- 4 cups fresh or canned peaches, sliced
- 1/2 cup granulated sugar
- 1 tablespoon lemon juice
- 1 cup all-purpose flour
- 1 cup granulated sugar
- 1 teaspoon baking powder
- 1/2 teaspoon salt
- 1 cup milk
- 1/2 cup unsalted butter, melted
- Ground cinnamon for dusting (optional)

Directions:

1. Flip down the toaster oven to the "Bake" mode.
2. Set the temperature to 375°F.
3. In a bowl, combine sliced peaches, sugar, and lemon juice. Let it sit for 15 minutes.
4. In another bowl, whisk together flour, sugar, baking powder, and salt.
5. Add milk and melted butter to the dry ingredients, stirring until smooth.
6. Pour the batter into a greased baking dish.
7. Spoon the peach mixture evenly over the batter.
8. Bake for 25-30 minutes or until the top is golden brown and bubbly.
9. Allow the peach cobbler to cool for a few minutes before serving.
10. Optionally, dust with ground cinnamon before serving.

Nutritional Value (Amount per Serving):

Calories: 325; Fat: 9.05; Carb: 61.5; Protein: 3.78

Raspberry Lemon Bars

Prep Time: 20 Minutes   Cook Time: 35 Minutes   Serves: 6

Ingredients:

- 1 cup all-purpose flour
- 1/2 cup unsalted butter, softened
- 1/4 cup powdered sugar
- 1 1/2 cups granulated sugar
- 1/4 cup all-purpose flour
- 4 large eggs
- Zest and juice of 2 lemons
- 1 cup fresh raspberries
- Powdered sugar for dusting

Directions:

1. Flip down the toaster oven to the "Bake" mode.
2. Set the temperature to 350°F.
3. In a bowl, combine flour, softened butter, and powdered sugar. Press into the bottom of a greased baking dish.

4. In another bowl, whisk together sugar, flour, eggs, lemon zest, and lemon juice until smooth.
5. Gently fold in the raspberries. Pour the filling over the crust.
6. Bake for 25-30 minutes or until the edges are set and the center is slightly jiggly.
7. Allow the bars to cool in the pan for 10 minutes, then transfer to a wire rack.
8. Dust with powdered sugar before slicing into bars.

Nutritional Value (Amount per Serving):

Calories: 382; Fat: 13.64; Carb: 60.87; Protein: 5.51

Peanut Butter Chocolate Brownies

Prep Time: 20 Minutes   Cook Time: 25 Minutes   Serves: 6

Ingredients:

- 1/2 cup unsalted butter
- 1 cup granulated sugar
- 2 large eggs
- 1 teaspoon vanilla extract
- 1/2 cup all-purpose flour
- 1/3 cup unsweetened cocoa powder
- 1/4 teaspoon baking powder
- 1/4 teaspoon salt
- 1/2 cup creamy peanut butter
- 1/2 cup chocolate chips

Directions:

1. Flip down the toaster oven to the "Bake" mode.
2. Set the temperature to 350°F.
3. In a saucepan, melt the butter. Remove from heat and stir in sugar, eggs, and vanilla extract.
4. In a separate bowl, whisk together flour, cocoa powder, baking powder, and salt.
5. Combine wet and dry ingredients until just mixed.
6. Pour the brownie batter into a greased baking dish.
7. Drop spoonfuls of peanut butter onto the batter and swirl with a knife.
8. Sprinkle chocolate chips over the top.
9. Bake for 20-25 minutes or until a toothpick inserted comes out with a few moist crumbs.
10. Allow the brownies to cool in the pan before cutting into squares.

Nutritional Value (Amount per Serving):

Calories: 356; Fat: 26.8; Carb: 39.39; Protein: 9.28

Raspberry Almond Tart

Prep Time: 30 Minutes   Cook Time: 25 Minutes   Serves: 8

Ingredients:

- 1 sheet of puff pastry, thawed
- 1/2 cup almond meal
- 1/4 cup granulated sugar
- 1/4 cup unsalted butter, melted
- 1 teaspoon almond extract
- 1 cup fresh raspberries
- Powdered sugar for dusting

Directions:

1. Flip down the toaster oven to the "Bake" mode.
2. Set the temperature to 375°F.
3. Roll out the puff pastry and place it in a tart pan.
4. In a bowl, mix almond meal, sugar, melted butter, and almond extract. Spread this mixture over the pastry.
5. Sprinkle fresh raspberries over the almond mixture.
6. Bake for 20-25 minutes or until the pastry is golden brown.
7. Allow the tart to cool before dusting with powdered sugar.

Nutritional Value (Amount per Serving):

Calories: 158; Fat: 9.41; Carb: 17.56; Protein: 1.58

Blueberry Lemon Scones

Prep Time: 15 Minutes   Cook Time: 20 Minutes   Serves: 8

Ingredients:

- 2 cups all-purpose flour
- 1/2 cup granulated sugar
- 1 tablespoon baking powder
- 1/2 teaspoon salt
- 1/2 cup unsalted butter, cold and cubed
- 1 cup fresh blueberries
- Zest of 1 lemon
- 2/3 cup heavy cream
- 1 teaspoon vanilla extract

Directions:

1. Flip down the toaster oven to the "Bake" mode.
2. Set the temperature to 400°F.
3. In a large bowl, whisk together flour, sugar, baking powder, and salt.
4. Cut in the cold butter until the mixture resembles coarse crumbs.
5. Gently fold in blueberries and lemon zest.
6. Stir in heavy cream and vanilla extract until just combined.
7. Turn the dough onto a floured surface, pat into a circle, and cut into 8 wedges.
8. Place the scones on a baking sheet and bake for 15-20 minutes until

golden.

9. Allow the scones to cool slightly before serving.

Nutritional Value (Amount per Serving):

Calories: 275; Fat: 11.87; Carb: 38.78; Protein: 4.13

Oatmeal Raisin Cookies

Prep Time: 15 Minutes   Cook Time: 12 Minutes   Serves: 24

Ingredients:

- 1 cup old-fashioned oats
- 3/4 cup all-purpose flour
- 1/2 teaspoon baking soda
- 1/2 teaspoon ground cinnamon
- 1/4 teaspoon salt
- 1/2 cup unsalted butter, softened
- 1/2 cup granulated sugar
- 1/2 cup packed brown sugar
- 1 large egg
- 1 teaspoon vanilla extract
- 1 cup raisins

Directions:

1. Flip down the toaster oven to the "Bake" mode.
2. Set the temperature to 350°F.
3. In a bowl, whisk together oats, flour, baking soda, cinnamon, and salt.
4. In another bowl, cream together butter, granulated sugar, and brown sugar until light and fluffy.
5. Beat in the egg and vanilla extract until well combined.
6. Gradually add the dry ingredients to the wet ingredients, mixing until just combined.
7. Stir in the raisins. Drop rounded tablespoons of dough onto a baking sheet.
8. Bake for 10-12 minutes or until the edges are golden.
9. Allow the cookies to cool on the baking sheet for 5 minutes before transferring to a wire rack to cool completely.

Nutritional Value (Amount per Serving):

Calories: 76; Fat: 3.07; Carb: 12.26; Protein: 1.36

Coconut Macaroons

Prep Time: 20 Minutes   Cook Time: 15 Minutes   Serves: 6

Ingredients:

- 3 cups shredded coconut
- 3/4 cup sweetened condensed milk
- 1 teaspoon vanilla extract

- 2 large egg whites
- 1/4 teaspoon salt
- Optional: Chocolate for dipping

Directions:

1. Flip down the toaster oven to the "Bake" mode.
2. Set the temperature to 325°F.
3. In a bowl, combine shredded coconut, sweetened condensed milk, and vanilla extract.
4. In another bowl, beat egg whites with salt until stiff peaks form.
5. Gently fold the egg whites into the coconut mixture.
6. Drop rounded tablespoons onto a baking sheet.
7. Bake for 12-15 minutes or until the edges are golden.
8. If desired, melt chocolate and dip the bottoms of the macaroons.
9. Allow the macaroons to cool on the baking sheet before serving.

Nutritional Value (Amount per Serving):

Calories: 89; Fat: 1.42; Carb: 15.31; Protein: 3.32

Pumpkin Bread

Prep Time: 15 Minutes   Cook Time: 45 Minutes   Serves: 6

Ingredients:

- 2 cups all-purpose flour
- 1 1/2 teaspoons baking powder
- 1/2 teaspoon baking soda
- 1/2 teaspoon salt
- 1 teaspoon ground cinnamon
- 1/2 teaspoon ground nutmeg
- 1/2 teaspoon ground cloves
- 1/2 cup unsalted butter, melted
- 1 cup granulated sugar
- 1/2 cup brown sugar, packed
- 2 large eggs
- 1 can (15 ounces) pumpkin puree
- 1 teaspoon vanilla extract

Directions:

1. Flip down the toaster oven to the "Bake" mode.
2. Set the temperature to 350°F.
3. In a bowl, whisk together flour, baking powder, baking soda, salt, cinnamon, nutmeg, and cloves.
4. In another bowl, cream together melted butter, granulated sugar, and brown sugar until smooth.
5. Beat in the eggs, one at a time, then add the pumpkin puree and vanilla extract.
6. Gradually add the dry ingredients to the wet ingredients, mixing until just combined.
7. Pour the batter into a greased loaf pan.

8. Bake for 40-45 minutes or until a toothpick inserted into the center comes out clean.
9. Allow the pumpkin bread to cool in the pan for 10 minutes before transferring to a wire rack to cool completely.

Nutritional Value (Amount per Serving):

Calories: 425; Fat: 12.53; Carb: 72.33; Protein: 7.04

Lemon Poppy Seed Muffins

Prep Time: 15 Minutes   Cook Time: 20 Minutes   Serves: 4-6

Ingredients:
- 2 cups all-purpose flour
- 1/2 cup granulated sugar
- 1 tablespoon poppy seeds
- 1 tablespoon baking powder
- 1/2 teaspoon baking soda
- 1/4 teaspoon salt
- 1 cup milk
- 1/2 cup unsalted butter, melted
- 2 tablespoons lemon juice
- Zest of 1 lemon
- 2 large eggs
- 1 teaspoon vanilla extract

Directions:
1. Flip down the toaster oven to the "Bake" mode.
2. Set the temperature to 375°F.
3. In a bowl, whisk together flour, sugar, poppy seeds, baking powder, baking soda, and salt.
4. In another bowl, whisk together milk, melted butter, lemon juice, lemon zest, eggs, and vanilla extract.
5. Gradually add the dry ingredients to the wet ingredients, mixing until just combined.
6. Spoon the batter into muffin cups, filling each about 2/3 full.
7. Bake for 15-20 minutes or until a toothpick inserted into the center comes out clean.
8. Allow the muffins to cool in the pan for 5 minutes, then transfer to a wire rack to cool completely.

Nutritional Value (Amount per Serving):

Calories: 402; Fat: 17.01; Carb: 53.8; Protein: 8.89

Chocolate Pudding Cake

Prep Time: 15 Minutes   Cook Time: 30 Minutes   Serves: 8

Ingredients:
- 1 cup all-purpose flour
- 1/2 cup granulated sugar

- 2 tablespoons cocoa powder
- 2 teaspoons baking powder
- 1/4 teaspoon salt
- 1/2 cup milk
- 1/4 cup unsalted butter, melted
- 1 teaspoon vanilla extract
- 1/2 cup packed brown sugar
- 1/4 cup cocoa powder
- 1 3/4 cups hot water

Directions:

1. Flip down the toaster oven to the "Bake" mode.
2. Set the temperature to 350°F.
3. In a bowl, whisk together flour, sugar, cocoa powder, baking powder, and salt.
4. In another bowl, mix together milk, melted butter, and vanilla extract.
5. Gradually add the dry ingredients to the wet ingredients, mixing until just combined.
6. Spread the batter in a greased baking dish.
7. In a small bowl, mix brown sugar and cocoa powder. Sprinkle this mixture over the batter.
8. Pour hot water over the entire mixture. Do not stir.
9. Bake for 25-30 minutes or until the center is set.
10. Allow the cake to cool slightly before serving. Serve warm with a scoop of ice cream if desired.

Nutritional Value (Amount per Serving):

Calories: 189; Fat: 5.04; Carb: 35.38; Protein: 3.07

Peanut Butter Banana Muffins

Prep Time: 15 Minutes   Cook Time: 20 Minutes   Serves: 6

Ingredients:

- 2 cups all-purpose flour
- 1/2 cup granulated sugar
- 1 tablespoon baking powder
- 1/2 teaspoon baking soda
- 1/4 teaspoon salt
- 3 ripe bananas, mashed
- 1/2 cup creamy peanut butter
- 1/4 cup unsalted butter, melted
- 2 large eggs
- 1 teaspoon vanilla extract
- 1/2 cup milk
- 1/2 cup chocolate chips (optional)

Directions:

1. Flip down the toaster oven to the "Bake" mode.
2. Set the temperature to 375°F.
3. In a bowl, whisk together flour, sugar, baking powder, baking soda, and salt.
4. In another bowl, combine mashed bananas, peanut butter, melted butter, eggs, vanilla extract, and milk.
5. Gradually add the dry ingredients to the wet ingredients, mixing until just

combined.
6. If using, fold in chocolate chips.
7. Spoon the batter into muffin cups, filling each about 2/3 full.
8. Bake for 15-20 minutes or until a toothpick inserted into the center comes out clean.
9. Allow the muffins to cool in the pan for 5 minutes, then transfer to a wire rack to cool completely.

Nutritional Value (Amount per Serving):

Calories: 533; Fat: 25.48; Carb: 66.73; Protein: 12.63

Apple Cranberry Crisp

Prep Time: 20 Minutes   Cook Time: 30 Minutes   Serves: 6

Ingredients:

- 4 cups peeled and sliced apples (such as Granny Smith)
- 1 cup fresh or frozen cranberries
- 1/2 cup granulated sugar
- 1 tablespoon all-purpose flour
- 1 teaspoon ground cinnamon
- 1/2 cup old-fashioned oats
- 1/4 cup all-purpose flour
- 1/4 cup brown sugar, packed
- 3 tablespoons unsalted butter, cold and cubed
- Vanilla ice cream (optional, for serving)

Directions:

1. Flip down the toaster oven to the "Bake" mode.
2. Set the temperature to 375°F.
3. In a bowl, combine sliced apples, cranberries, granulated sugar, 1 tablespoon flour, and cinnamon. Toss until fruit is coated.
4. In another bowl, mix oats, 1/4 cup flour, brown sugar, and cubed cold butter until crumbly.
5. Transfer the fruit mixture to a greased baking dish.
6. Sprinkle the crumble topping evenly over the fruit.
7. Bake for 25-30 minutes or until the topping is golden brown, and the fruit is bubbly.
8. Allow the crisp to cool for a few minutes before serving. Top with a scoop of vanilla ice cream if desired.

Nutritional Value (Amount per Serving):

Calories: 307; Fat: 5.03; Carb: 68.31; Protein: 3.11

Cherry Almond Galette

Prep Time: 20 Minutes   Cook Time: 30 Minutes   Serves: 6

Ingredients:

- 1 sheet of refrigerated pie crust or homemade pie crust
- 2 cups fresh or frozen cherries, pitted
- 1/4 cup granulated sugar
- 1 tablespoon cornstarch
- 1/2 teaspoon almond extract
- 2 tablespoons sliced almonds
- 1 tablespoon milk (for brushing the crust)
- Powdered sugar (for dusting, optional)

Directions:

1. Flip down the toaster oven to the "Bake" mode.
2. Set the temperature to 375°F.
3. In a bowl, combine cherries, granulated sugar, cornstarch, and almond extract. Toss until cherries are coated.
4. Roll out the pie crust on a parchment-lined baking sheet.
5. Spoon the cherry mixture onto the center of the pie crust, leaving about a 2-inch border.
6. Sprinkle sliced almonds over the cherries.
7. Gently fold the edges of the pie crust over the filling, creating a rustic edge.
8. Brush the edges of the crust with milk.
9. Bake for 25-30 minutes or until the crust is golden brown and the filling is bubbly.
10. Allow the galette to cool for a few minutes before serving. Dust with powdered sugar if desired.

Nutritional Value (Amount per Serving):

Calories: 272; Fat: 9.91; Carb: 44.91; Protein: 2.31

APPENDIX RECIPE INDEX

A
Apple Cinnamon Baked Oatmeal ·················· 97
Apple Cranberry Crisp ································· 107
Apple Walnut Breakfast Bread ······················ 24
Apricot Glazed Chicken Drumettes ·············· 37
Avocado and Black Bean Quesadillas ··········· 84
Avocado Toast with Poached Eggs ················ 22

B
Bacon-Wrapped Jalapeño Poppers ················ 85
Bagel Salmon Avocado Toast ························ 61
Baked Banana Nut Oatmeal ·························· 26
Baked Mediterranean Vegetables with Quinoa ·· 66
Baked Zucchini Fries ···································· 86
Balsamic-Glazed Beef Skewers ······················ 51
Banana Nut Muffins ····································· 96
Banana Walnut Muffins ································ 30
BBQ Chicken Flatbread ································ 90
Berry Crumble ·· 95
Berry-Stuffed French Toast ··························· 22
Blackened Red Snapper Tacos ······················· 60
Blueberry Almond Baked Oatmeal ················ 29
Blueberry Almond Breakfast Bread ··············· 23
Blueberry Lemon Scones ····························· 102
Breakfast Pizza ·· 30
Broccoli and Cheddar Stuffed Potatoes ········· 74
Bruschetta with Balsamic Glaze ···················· 92
Buffalo Cauliflower Bites ······························ 83
Butternut Squash and Sage Risotto ··············· 76

C
Cajun Baked Catfish ····································· 56
Cajun Catfish Po' Boys ·································· 63
Caprese Skewers ·· 82
Caprese Stuffed Chicken Roll-Ups ················ 39
Caprese Stuffed Portobello Mushrooms ········ 69
Caramelized Onion and Gruyere Tart ··········· 78
Cauliflower and Chickpea Curry ··················· 71
Cheesy Garlic Bread Bites ····························· 81
Cherry Almond Galette ······························· 108
Chicken Club Casseroles ······························· 33

Chipotle Pork Enchiladas ······························ 51
Chocolate Chip Cookies ································ 95
Chocolate Pudding Cake ····························· 105
Cinnamon French Toast Sticks ······················ 28
Cinnamon Sugar Donuts ······························· 99
Coconut Curry Chicken Drumsticks ············· 36
Coconut Macaroons ···································· 103
Coconut Shrimp with Mango Salsa ··············· 59
Cranberry Pecan Stuffed Chicken Thighs ····· 41
Crispy Baked Chicken Wings ························ 35
Crispy Baked Fish Tacos ······························· 57
Crispy Baked Parmesan Chicken Breasts ······ 40
Crispy Garlic Parmesan Baked Cod ·············· 60
Crispy Parmesan Baked Chicken Tenders ····· 37
Cuban-Style Mojo Pork Skewers ··················· 50
Cucumber Bites with Dill Cream Cheese ······ 88

E
Eggplant Parmesan ·· 77

F
French Onion Beef Sliders ···························· 45

G
Garlic Butter Shrimp Skewers ······················· 55
Golden Chicken Cordon Bleu ······················· 33
Greek Salad Skewers ····································· 89
Greek Spanakopita Triangles ························· 91

H
Herb-Crusted Beef Baguette Sandwich ········· 47
Herb-Crusted Lamb Chops ··························· 44
Honey Glazed Baked Ham ···························· 45
Honey Mustard Glazed Turkey Breast ·········· 34
Honey Soy Glazed Chicken Thighs ··············· 40

I
Italian-Style Baked Meatballs ························ 43

L
Lamb and Vegetable Kebabs ························· 46
Lemon Blueberry Pound Cake ······················ 97
Lemon Dill Baked Whole Branzino ··············· 56
Lemon Herb Baked Salmon ·························· 55
Lemon Herb Broiled Scallops ······················· 62

Lemon Poppy Seed Muffins ... 105
Lemon-Honey Glazed Lamb Ribs ... 52
Lentil Loaf ... 81

M
Mango Habanero Baked Halibut ... 62
Mango-Glazed Pork Chops ... 48
Maple Mustard Glazed Chicken Thighs ... 39
Maple Pecan Baked French Toast ... 27
Mediterranean Chicken and Vegetable Skewers 38
Mediterranean Pita Nachos ... 93
Mediterranean Shakshuka ... 31
Mediterranean Stuffed Mini Peppers ... 87
Mediterranean Stuffed Sole ... 58
Mediterranean Stuffed Squid ... 64
Mini Cheesecakes ... 98
Mini Margherita Pizzas ... 83
Mini Meatball Sliders ... 84
Mini Shrimp Tacos ... 90
Mint and Garlic Marinated Lamb Kebabs ... 49
Moroccan Lamb Meatball Tagine ... 50

O
Oatmeal Raisin Cookies ... 103
Oven-Baked BBQ Pork Ribs ... 44

P
Peach Cobbler ... 100
Peanut Butter Banana Muffins ... 106
Peanut Butter Chocolate Brownies ... 101
Pesto Baked Tilapia ... 57
Pesto Baked Veggie Wrap ... 67
Pesto Stuffed Chicken Breasts ... 36
Pizza Stuffed Mushrooms ... 89
Pomegranate Glazed Turkey Meatballs ... 41
Pork and Apple Quesadillas ... 52
Pork and Apple Stuffed Acorn Squash ... 46
Pork and Veggie Stir-Fry ... 49
Pumpkin Bread ... 104

Q
Quinoa and Black Bean Stuffed Bell Peppers ... 72

R
Raspberry Almond Tart ... 102
Raspberry Lemon Bars ... 100
Ratatouille ... 73
Red Pepper Hummus ... 85

S
Sesame-Crusted Ahi Tuna ... 63
Smashed Avocado and Tomato Toast ... 26
Smoked Salmon Bagel ... 29
Southwest Quinoa Stuffed Peppers ... 91
Spicy BBQ Beef Tacos ... 53
Spicy Broiled Shrimp Tostadas ... 61
Spinach and Feta Breakfast Wrap ... 23
Spinach and Feta Stuffed Chicken Breasts ... 38
Spinach and Ricotta Stuffed Shells ... 73
Spinach and Stuffed Portobello Mushrooms ... 66
Spinach Beef Pie ... 43
Stuffed Bell Peppers with Ground Beef ... 48
Stuffed Bell Peppers with Lentils and Brown Rice ... 68
Stuffed Jalapeño Popper Dip ... 88
Sweet and Sour Pineapple Pork ... 47
Sweet Potato and Black Bean Enchiladas ... 75
Sweet Potato and Black Bean Quesadillas ... 68

T
Teriyaki Chicken Skewers ... 87
Teriyaki Glazed Salmon Skewers ... 58
Teriyaki Tofu and Vegetable Skewers ... 78
Turkey Meat Loaf ... 34

V
Veggie and Quinoa Stuffed Bell Peppers ... 75
Veggie Breakfast Burritos ... 24
Veggie Omelette Muffins ... 25
Veggie Pesto Pasta Bake ... 70
Veggie-packed Frittata ... 27

Z
Zucchini Noodles with Pesto and Cherry Tomatoes ... 71

Printed in Dunstable, United Kingdom